The Slow Road

The Slow Road

The Complete Guide to Van Life in New Zealand

Kirianna and Lachlan Poole

ALLEN&UNWIN
AUCKLAND · SYDNEY · MELBOURNE · LONDON

Contents

Map of New Zealand	6
About us	9
BEFORE YOU GO	**15**
Getting a van	16
Shipping a vehicle to New Zealand	20
Getting ready to go	24
Being prepared	34
Finding work while travelling	42
Camping life	44
Travelling with kids	48
Must-have apps	54
ON THE ROAD	**57**
NORTH ISLAND	**59**
Northland/Te Tai Tokerau	61
Auckland/Tāmaki Makaurau	79
Waikato	94
Bay of Plenty/Te Moana-a-Toi	119
Gisborne/Te Tairāwhiti	143
Hawke's Bay/Te Matau-a-Māui	149
Taranaki	157
Manawatū-Whanganui	163
Wellington/Te Whanganui-a-Tara	173
SOUTH ISLAND	**183**
Marlborough/Te Tauihu-o-te-Waka	185
Nelson Tasman/Whakatū	193
West Coast/Te Tai Poutini	207
Canterbury/Waitaha	225
Otago/Ōtākou	265
Southland/Murihiku	301
Goodbye, New Zealand	310
This is for you	312
Index	314

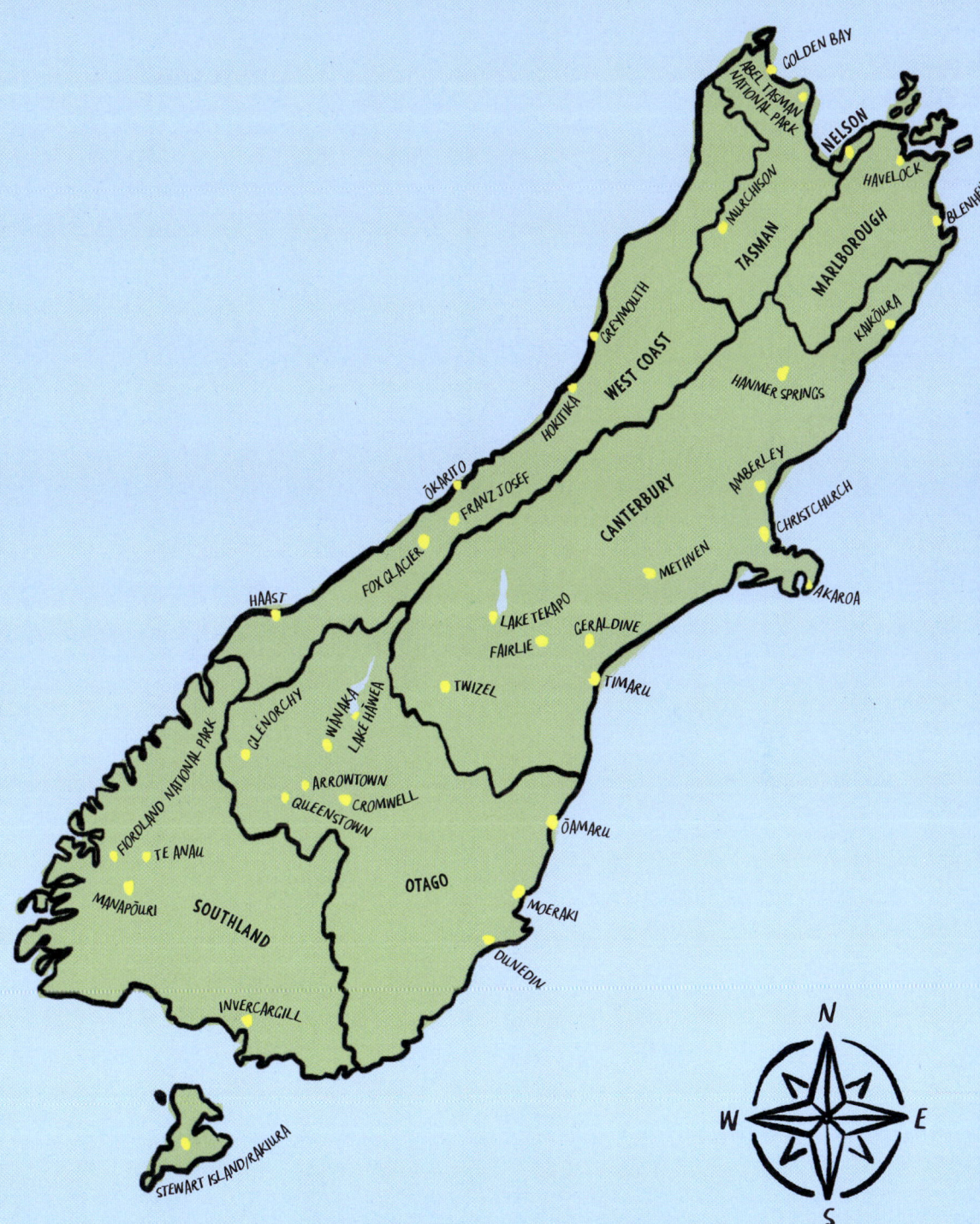

About us

My name is Kiri, and I am a proud Māori woman from Te Whānau-ā-Apanui. I was raised in New Zealand by my beautiful and kind grandparents. We often went on road trips together and I spent many holidays during my childhood camping at the beach under the shade of pōhutukawa trees, and fishing with my cousins along the East Coast. These experiences in nature are some of my most treasured memories and they fed my passion for adventure and spontaneity.

In 2012, I met a man named Lockie who shares these passions and he became my husband. We both believe in living life to the fullest and taking the adventurous route through life. Lockie also has fond childhood memories of camping in his grandparents' van, 'Queenie', and chasing waves on the mid-north coast of New South Wales, Australia.

Lockie and I enjoy escaping to new places whenever we can. In 2014, we made the bold decision to embark on an adventure and move from Auckland to Japan. During our first few years there, we learned a lot about Japanese culture, which inspired us to embrace minimalism and simplicity. Living in a small Japanese apartment taught us to be creative with our space and truly appreciate the little things. We learned to live with less and enjoy time together rather than chasing after material possessions.

In 2016, exciting changes came our way. Lockie and I were thrilled to be expecting our first baby. At 37 weeks pregnant, I took a flight to Sydney to give birth to our son, Riley. After spending a few months in Australia, Riley and I headed back to Japan — but that was only the start of our adventures together as a family. With our little one in tow, we embarked on a non-stop journey that took us through 37 countries before Riley's first birthday.

However, we soon felt the urge to return to our home countries. We wanted Riley to learn about his heritage, history and culture. But most importantly, we wanted to be together as a family and spend quality time with one another.

At the same time, Lockie and I wanted to explore Australia and New Zealand more deeply. Our goal has always been to embrace parenthood on the road with our children. As a mother, I wanted to pass on the spirit of exploration and the love of nature to our children, just as my own childhood memories had inspired me.

We planned to travel around both countries, starting with Australia. Lockie had always dreamed of owning a Volkswagen split-screen Kombi, which has dual windscreens that pop open to enjoy the breeze on a hot day, and multiple windows along the body, making the interior bright and light. The prospect of van life suited the spirit of minimalism we had learned in Japan.

We spent months watching online car sales and looking through vintage car forums. Finally, we heard that a family friend was selling his Kombi in Perth and we were enchanted by the images we saw. Within a week, we were test-driving the bus, and the owner suggested we take it away for a few days to the Margaret River region. We fell so in love with the Kombi that we couldn't imagine our lives without her. The van was perfect for our slow style of travel as we wanted to take it easy and spend our days on the beach. It was also great for Riley, as he could take in everything as we drove by.

We returned to Perth feeling overjoyed at the thought of buying the Kombi. During our chat with the owner, we shared our wild plans to explore the country and expressed our love for the van. Sadly, though, we were still a long way off the asking price and he just couldn't accept the offer we made. We felt terribly disappointed and spent the night heartbroken.

But the very next day, the owner called us. He had slept on it and had a change of heart. He loved our plans to embark on a big adventure with the Kombi and he wanted it to go to a good home. He agreed to drop the price. We were ecstatic. Tears of joy streamed down our faces when we became the proud owners of 'Izzie', as I named her that afternoon.

We spent many nights — with a glass of wine in our hands — planning and dreaming of how we could travel around Australia. We were drawn to the thought of red dirt, pastel-blue water and quiet evenings around the campfire. As new parents, we also wanted to fully enjoy Riley's early years together, exploring beautiful places with fewer distractions and giving him our undivided attention.

Kicking up dust in Australia

After we spent a few months fitting out the van, we started our journey, heading clockwise around the huge country. We quickly became accustomed to our travelling lifestyle, experiencing anything and everything that came our way, often driving with open windows and the sound of the beach calling us. We learned so much in those early days: how to properly pack for a road trip, what our favourite road-trip snacks were, how to cook in the great outdoors and how to camp with a baby.

We thoroughly enjoyed spending quality time together, showing Riley the beauty of his home country and living with fewer distractions compared to our busy lives in Japan.

By 2019, after 18 months on the road, we had explored much of Australia, including small islands and many charming out-of-the-way places, fallen

in love with numerous beaches and made wonderful friends. But we were now eagerly awaiting the arrival of our second child in June of that year. We made our way from Darwin to the Gold Coast as quickly as possible to welcome our daughter, Alba, into the world.

We stopped for seven months to enjoy the baby bubble and settled in the little surf town of Lennox Head in New South Wales, but still visiting nearby areas for mini-adventures in our Kombi.

Covid strikes

The Covid-19 pandemic was a major disruption in everyone's life and for us it meant the challenges of uncertain work and strict restrictions of travel — especially overseas. We decided to take it as an opportunity to show Alba the life Riley had lived during our experiences on the road. We made a few changes to Izzie as we couldn't all fit sleeping inside anymore, so we built an annex, bought some airbeds and put all of our belongings in storage. We began our second lap of Australia by travelling to the far north of Queensland just after the first Australian lockdown ended.

It was an unreal feeling to be back out exploring. As restrictions eased, we explored further and further, making our way back down the east coast onto Tasmania then through the dead centre of Australia, picnicking at Uluru, looping back to Western Australia and then through the Nullarbor to South Australia, before arriving back on the east coast. We faced some challenges along the way, such as driving without air conditioning, daily pack-ups and pack-downs, uncomfortable airbeds, schooling a five-year-old and being pregnant — again! However, we enjoyed spending time together and making new friends with other travelling families. We thought this was a temporary life, so we soaked in every minute. Riley and Alba had experiences I am sure they will never forget, like learning to fish for barramundi, spotting crocodiles in the wild, trekking around the Kimberley and learning about ancient Aboriginal traditions.

Despite the threat of Covid-19, we felt safe in our own little bubble. For us, the blessing in disguise was that by Christmas 2022 we were celebrating the upcoming arrival of our next little girl. However, we realised that three kids were a little too much for the Kombi and so we began searching for a solution. Lockie found a pink fibreglass 1964 Franklin caravan for sale while we were travelling through Western Australia. Although it required a full restoration and many upgrades, we were excited about the possibilities so we bought it and shipped it across to the East Coast.

The ultimate Kiwi road trip

Just days before the arrival of Elsie, our second daughter, the caravan arrived. We needed to reduce its weight and make sure it met all of the New Zealand self-contained standards, so Lockie spent eight weeks stripping it back and restoring it. At the same time, Izzie got a bigger engine and gearbox to be able to tow the caravan. Life felt so different to what it was in a little tent. We now had our own beds and a small kitchen and although extremely simple, it was all we needed. Our ambitions could now go beyond Australia.

My dream was to take my family travelling around New Zealand. It has always been important to me that my children experience their Kiwi heritage and, most importantly, spend time with my family in New Zealand. The freedom and wilderness were calling me. I wanted to camp under snow-capped mountains and next to still freshwater lakes as a family. New Zealand is so different to Australia and we were ready for some cooler air — and so was our air-cooled Kombi! We had talked about going over there with our Kombi for many years, so it came as no surprise when we shared the news with our loved ones.

In December 2022, we transported Izzie and the caravan from Australia to New Zealand by ship and the pair arrived in Auckland four weeks later. That's when we began our great Kiwi road trip through Aotearoa. We had no end in sight, just excitement and the open road ahead.

Our time here has been filled with heart-happy moments, peaceful campfire nights, conscious food, snow-capped mountains and exciting adventures. Throughout these pages, you'll find our advice, compiled over a year and a half of full-time travelling, including tips for making the most out of your road-trip adventures, some of my favourite recipes and places to see that have been memorable for our family. New Zealand is a place where mountainous ranges fall into the sea, where sustainable living is encouraged and our hearts feel full. I hope the experience of travelling Aotearoa brings you as much joy and fulfillment as it has brought my family. Travel safe — haere pai atu, hoki pai mai.

BEFORE YOU GO

Getting a van

DIY van builds have taken over YouTube, and if you have the time to put in the hours, along with a knack for building, then this could be an option. However, after establishing what kind of van suits your travel needs, taking into account your family size and cooking, bathroom and power needs, you may find that buying new or second-hand is a better option.

New campervans will have all the bells and whistles and will meet all current regulations, so you can just hit the road. Ex-rental and second-hand vans pop up for sale all the time, and you may find one that has the fitout you need for your van-life journey. The beauty of these options is just putting the keys in the ignition. However, they come at a cost and, most likely, ex-rentals will have very high mileage, so you will need to get a thorough mechanical check before buying.

Another thing to watch out for is whether the van has a current self-contained authorisation sticker (see pages 18–19).

Hiring a van
If you want to take a shorter trip or not fully commit to van life just yet, you can look at hiring a camper suitable for your next adventure. There are a number of rental car/camper/motorhome companies in New Zealand, with a fleet to suit almost all budgets and comfort requirements.

Camplify
Camplify is a peer-to-peer vehicle rental service, making it easier for you to experience van life at a reasonable cost. Camplify takes advantage of the underuse of many vans and motorhomes by connecting you with campers and caravans in your neighbourhood or in other parts of New Zealand.

You can choose from a wide range of vehicles, from luxury motorhomes with all the mod cons to a more affordable camper trailer. Some vehicles are also available for a longer-term hire.

Travellers Autobarn
Travellers Autobarn is a campervan-hire company that caters to backpackers and budget travellers. They offer a range of factory-built and custom-modified campervans, and are one of the most affordable options for exploring New Zealand, particularly during the off-peak season. They have a variety of models to choose from.

Apollo
Apollo have a great reputation. Choose from self-contained motorhomes with all the bells and whistles, or take the

less-frills route with a compact camper for an authentic van-life experience.

Maui
Maui campers are seen everywhere throughout New Zealand. With plenty of inside space and modern features, you can enjoy the comforts of home while on the road.

JUCY
JUCY rentals are aimed at the budget end of the market, but various vehicle types are available to suit different preferences. JUCY is a great choice for a couple or solo traveller, as the vans are smaller for camping in those cute little nooks of New Zealand. The basic models are not self-contained, but larger vans can accommodate up to four people and come equipped with a cassette toilet, grey-water tank and other amenities.

Legal requirements
If your caravan or van weighs less than 3500 kg, it will need to have a warrant of fitness (WOF) in order to legally drive it on the road. However, if you have a larger vehicle like a campervan that exceeds 3500 kg, you will require a Certificate of Fitness (COF) instead. These documents can be obtained from VTNZ, which is located in almost all major towns in New Zealand. New Zealand Motor Caravan Association (NZMCA) members receive a substantial discount on the cost of these inspections.

When buying a caravan or van, VTNZ can also help with pre-purchase inspection. This should reveal any issues with the vehicle and ensure you have all the facts you need to make the right decision.

It is also mandatory for your vehicle to have an electrical warrant of fitness (EWOF). Caravan parks will request to see the EWOF upon check-in, before you can connect to the 230-volt supply system. This warrant can only be issued by a registered electrical inspector. You will then receive a copy of the EWOF form, along with an identifying sticker for the vehicle window that serves as proof of compliance.

Freedom camping and being 'self contained'
The idea of 'freedom camping', away from commercial camping sites, is popular with many adventurers building their dream van. They are drawn to the idea of escaping the rat race in search of making memories in the mountains, by rugged shorelines and untamed forests. There are many places in New Zealand where you can camp overnight in public areas instead of a managed campsite. However, knowing the rules and restrictions of freedom camping is essential to avoid any trouble. New legislation was passed in 2023, with updated rules coming into force. Check the NZMCA website for updates, and

look at local council websites for each area you are travelling to, to make sure you have the most up-to-date information.

A certified self-contained camper has to meet its occupants' ablutionary (washing and toileting) needs for up to three days, without external services or waste discharge. The following are the main requirements for a vehicle to be certified as self-contained:

- freshwater tank capable of carrying 12 litres of drinking water per person (4 litres a day for three days)
- vented grey/black water tank
- fixed toilet (mandatory for new builds), with sufficient capacity for three days
- sink, connected to wastewater tank with a hose with smell trap
- rubbish bin with a lid.

An authorised certifier — such as the NZMCA (www.nzmca.org.nz) or NZ Lifestyle Camping (www.nzlifestylecamping.com) — will carry out an inspection of the van's water tanks, plumbing, toilet system and discharge hoses. Once approved, your vehicle will be provided with an SCNZ sticker.

Shipping a vehicle to New Zealand

For us, bringing our Kombi and caravan across from Australia was a no-brainer. We had a complete setup and didn't want to purchase everything new again once we arrived in New Zealand.

After some research, we discovered the Carnet de Passages en Douane (CPD), which is basically a passport for your vehicle and enables you to drive through numerous countries using your own vehicle on your current registration. The CPD means Customs doesn't need to hold an import deposit, and guarantees the country you are entering that the vehicle will be exported within the applicable timeframe. The CPD is valid for 12 months, with a possibility of a further 12-month extension. Your vehicle must have current registration in your country of origin throughout your overseas trip. Numerous countries around the world are part of the Carnet de Passages agreement, so you can adventure far and wide if that's what your heart desires!

You can apply for the CPD through your local motor club (for us the Australian Automobile Association). The process is a little tricky, and we had to do quite a few things to get our CPD approved: get valuations of both vehicles, schedule a paperwork check, and make payment (around AU$1570 per vehicle, with $500 being returned when the vehicle returns to Australia).

Once approved, the next step is preparing your vehicle for departure. As you can imagine, biosecurity regulations mean the vehicle has to be spotless, and I mean *spotless*! We pulled the entire Kombi and caravan apart, vacuuming, scrubbing and scrubbing some more. If you are like us and have kids, you will find some mouldy apples under the seats at the very least, but it was so good to see the Kombi sparkle inside and out. It didn't end there — everything we were taking to New Zealand needed to be deep-cleaned: pots and pans, fishing rods, boots and shoes. We parked at my mother-in-law's and went for it over three full days.

Shipping

Shipping companies vary in what they offer and the ports they operate from. To ensure you get the best deal, call around and compare quotes. In our case, we used Dolphin Shipping, departing from Wollongong and arriving into Auckland, and opted for a roll-on and roll-off service. However, containers are also available as an option.

It's nerve-wracking handing over your pride and joy and hoping it doesn't get damaged on the voyage. You can purchase insurance for the crossing at an extra cost, and we decided it was worth the peace of mind. Both the

Kombi and caravan arrived in perfect condition, with no damage whatsoever. Dolphin covered the following services:
- managing ocean freight
- handling import customs clearance upon arrival
- overseeing inspection by the Ministry for Primary Industries (MPI)
- coordinating New Zealand border inspection.

We could track the ship's progress, and it was pretty cool to watch and wait. Due to Christmas and bad weather, the boat ended up being delayed, with a total time from drop-off to pick-up of four weeks — two weeks over the estimated time. Once in Auckland, the processing time was about another eight days. Our broker advised us that most vehicles get stopped and require extra cleaning, for which there would be an additional charge and a few more days' delay. Our thorough scrubbing must have paid off, though, as both the Kombi and caravan were cleared first go. We were free! We celebrated with a trip to Waiheke Island.

Biosecurity

When importing a vehicle into New Zealand, it is essential to check all the items you are carrying in your caravan or van to avoid any delays due to customs and biosecurity regulations. When packing for our trip, we made sure that our caravan was loaded with the kids' bikes, camping gear, clothing and bedding. We also took great care to clean everything, including our boots, fishing gear and even the bike tires to prevent the transfer of soil, plant material, pests and seeds that can pose a threat to the environment and wildlife in New Zealand, as well as to agriculture. Failure to comply with these regulations can result in fines and delayed entry while Customs carries out a clean (and charges you a fee).

Be very careful if you are carrying any equipment, such as all hiking and sporting footwear, and any footwear that has been used outside urban areas. Camping equipment, hunting gear, backpacks, fishing and water-activity equipment (such as diving equipment and wetsuits, waders, fishing rods, lines, hooks and flies) should also be thoroughly checked and cleaned before entering New Zealand.

Getting ready to go

The first step towards hitting the road, whether it's for a few weeks or long term, is to have a plan. One way is to start with an idea of where you're headed and work back from there. But at the same time, have an open mind and remember that things can happen on the road, and you may end up on a detour. While New Zealand is a small country, there are a few things to consider when planning where to go and what to do.

Most international travellers arrive or start from Auckland or Christchurch, as these are the main international airports, but if you are based in New Zealand you already have a starting point! You will need to decide whether to do the North or South Islands, or both, and in what order. It's not quite as simple as driving in a circle around Australia!

New Zealand really does have something for everyone: adventurers after an intrepid nature hike, adrenaline junkies, snow enthusiasts, those into fishing, travellers who want to learn about culture and history or, like us, those keen on camping in the wilderness. Make a wish-list and start working out how to tick it off.

Tip
When I'm in the planning phase, I like to make a travel journal, filling it with ideas, weather, destinations, hot spots and activities suitable for the whole family. I compile everything neatly into categories, making it easy to reference. We also use a hard-copy map to help us visualise our destination and map out our journey more effectively.

Planning
Timeline
To ensure a smooth and well-planned trip, it's a good idea to establish a clear timeline with specific start and end dates. Then you have some basic parameters to work to.

Carefully consider the season in which you are travelling; many places are closed or have restricted hours outside the peak summer months. Having said that, we avoid peak seasons in certain areas, especially as the camp spots tend to fill up, making it hard to find a place for the night.

In New Zealand, weather-related road closures do happen, and not just in winter. When you're on the road, make sure you check regularly for updates, and plan for journeys to take extra time in wet or snowy conditions. The New Zealand Transport Agency (www.nzta.govt.nz) updates its website daily with information on roadworks, delays, closures and other warnings.

Weather and seasons

Our motto is 'Move with the weather'. Due to some pretty extreme weather in early 2023, we found ourselves zig-zagging around the North Island in order to avoid the worst and find the best of the weather.

New Zealand's weather can be unpredictable, and can throw up four seasons in one day. Travelling during the warmer months is best, as we enjoy living outside barefoot, but our experiences in New Zealand have taught us always to have our jackets and Uggs ready, as the weather can change quickly.

Having a clear idea of what the weather is going to do is essential, so research the weather patterns for the time of your trip. We regularly check Google Weather for a basic indication, and when things really close in we use the MetService website (www.metservice.com), which is handy and usually pretty accurate.

The country has many beautiful beaches — I'm currently camping opposite one as I write this — which is a good reason to travel in summer. In the south, the winter months often have glorious clear days with cold nights — so for snow-lovers keen on a breathtakingly pretty winter campout, there are plenty of options for outdoor fun despite the colder temperatures.

Once we have moved into the warmer months I pack up our winter gear and post it to my grandparents, to save on caravan storage.

Packing

After spending six years living in Tokyo, transitioning to caravan life was seamless. The Japanese have mastered the art of minimalistic living, which includes camping and packing. I am often inspired by Japanese minimalism, which values simplicity and keeping only what you need.

When selecting items for your camper, consider their functionality and how well they can be packed away. During our fitout, we sourced camping gear that was multi-purpose, durable, compact and long-lasting, and our favourite items continue to serve us well. Here are my recommendations for the essentials.

Kitchen gear

When selecting gear to fitout your camper, the abundance of options can make the process feel overwhelming. In my experience, it's best to keep things simple and lightweight. Go for compact pots and pans that stack together to save space. (Kathmandu offers a set that we love.) Our cast-iron skillet and camp oven are used religiously; they are simple to clean and care for, and with them we can make many beautiful meals.

Chopping boards are handy, as they can also serve as platters. We prefer bamboo and wooden chopping boards to avoid using plastic, plus they are more durable and aesthetically pleasing.

Enamel plates are durable and stack

well. Make sure you have a full set of knives and forks so you can cover for any that get lost or cater for guests along the way. (Check out second-hand stores and op shops — they often have cool vintage stuff for peanuts.) I'd recommend having two decent kitchen knives — using a table knife to cut an onion can be frustrating.

My favourites when it comes to cups are ones that are easy to stack and insulated, to keep beverages at the perfect temperature, hot or cold. I mainly use Pottery for the Planet. Their bowls come with silicone lids that fit snugly over the top, providing an airtight seal to keep leftover food fresh.

Stop items from sliding around when you're on the road by lining your drawers and cupboards with non-stick mats that you can buy in rolls from dollar stores.

I have four key appliances in the caravan: a mini air fryer, a blender, a hand mixer and a coffee machine, as we all love smoothies and making our own sauces. The air fryer is compact and super-practical to use on the road. Our Smeg blender is nice and small, and comes with drinking cups. The mixer is a KitchenAid with a rechargeable battery, and we have a small pod coffee machine — because coffee is life.

Tips
- Find second-hand stores that sell pretty vintage mismatched plates, cups, cookware and cutlery.
- Rub a cut lemon on your kitchen boards to deodorise them.

Bedding and linen

New Zealand can get cold, especially for those enjoying the South Island during the winter months. Temperatures drop below zero in some areas, and depending on your van's insulation it can get pretty cold inside, too. It is a great idea to have back-up bedding, like a sleeping bag, stashed away.

Our kids loved using 12-volt electric blankets when we camped in the snow, but nothing beats a good old hot-water bottle.

Food

Everyone needs good food, and having a well-stocked pantry is key to happy campers. There is nothing worse than arriving somewhere late and having to rummage for food. My biggest travel tips are always having snacks at hand, and having some pre-made meals in the freezer ready to defrost.

Though I encourage supporting small towns and purchasing local produce, opposite are some items I always have ready to go in the van or caravan.

Refrigerator	Freezer	Pantry
Dairy items, e.g. cottage cheese, milk, butter, yoghurt (including kids' yoghurt pouches)	Bulk-made meals, e.g. chicken for fajitas, teriyaki chicken, beef stroganoff, meatballs, smash patties for burgers	Tinned goods, e.g. anchovies, coconut milk, tomatoes, beans and legumes, tuna
Hummus	Ice cream	Bread and bread rolls
Eggs	Frozen vegetables, e.g. spinach, peas, edamame beans	Olive oil, sesame oil and rapeseed oil
Avocado		Pasta, e.g. spaghetti, curly noodles
Smoked salmon	Frozen fruits, e.g. blueberries, mango, chunks of banana	Sauces and condiments, e.g. hot chipotle, mustard, miso paste, tomato paste
Roast chicken		
Ham		Wholemeal wraps and tacos
Mayonnaise		
Fresh salad vegetables		Rice (microwavable), including brown rice, quinoa and couscous
Vegetables and fruit		
Proteins/meat for main meals		Flour (00 and all-purpose)
Medjool dates		Crackers, e.g. rice crackers, grain crackers, corn thins
		Nut mixtures
		Spices, e.g. paprika, all spice, chilli flakes, salt and pepper, dried herbs
		Protein powder
		Peanut butter, Vegemite, Marmite, jams, honey and preserves
		Jars of olives, peppers and pickles
		Stocks and vinegar

Healthy road-trip food ideas

When travelling with kids, snacks can be a great way to keep the kids happy and distracted. However, buying food from service stations or dairies along the way can add up, so we like to load up our kids' bento boxes each day to save money while keeping them satisfied. We recommend Love Mae bento-style lunchboxes because they are easy to stack in the caravan fridge but have plenty of space inside. Below are some great lunchbox ideas:

- corn thins, which are perfect for spreading and dipping
- Vegemite and cheese Cruskits
- boiled eggs
- pesto pasta salad
- veggie sticks and hummus
- sushi.

Wraps and sandwiches:
- breakfast wrap: make an egg omelette and pop it into a wrap, adding bacon, relish and spinach
- peanut butter and cinnamon
- chicken and mayo salad: mix shredded chicken with diced celery, cucumber and Kewpie mayo, then pop it into your bread of choice, with cos lettuce on either side to prevent the bread from turning soggy (the chicken and mayo mix is also good with almonds)
- tuna and mayo with dill
- Japanese egg (*tamago sando*) — egg mashed with Kewpie mayonnaise on white bread
- salmon and cream cheese with cucumber
- bacon and egg roll
- jambon baguette (I am a sucker for a French stick caked with butter and filled with prosciutto and cheese).

Salad jars:
- quinoa protein jar: veggies, a cup of quinoa and shredded chicken or tuna
- brekkie jar: kale, smoked salmon, hummus, poached eggs and quinoa
- miso noodles: precooked soba noodles, edamame beans, sesame, tofu, carrot and sprouts (and mix a tablespoon of miso paste with sesame oil, mirin, lime juice and soy sauce as a dressing)
- pasta curls: the kids love this — precooked curly pasta, feta, pinenuts, rocket, chicken and lots of olive oil
- chia: blend any fruits with coconut milk/water and choice of sweetener (we use honey). Blend until smooth then fold into a cup of chia seeds. Rest overnight and top with fresh fruit (and our kids also like whipped cream on top).
- chicken teriyaki: rice, avocado, teriyaki chicken, edamame beans, sesame seeds, nori and Kewpie mayo.

Sweet treats:
- bounty balls
- date bars
- peanut-butter crispies.

For more road-trip meal ideas, check out my book *The Slow Road Cookbook*.

Meal planning

To make meal planning simple, I have created a two-week plan for my family of five. Our goal is to eat nutritious and high-protein meals that keep us full.

I like to have a prep day to make as much food as I can in advance. I'll make batches of dishes like Mexican ground beef and chicken fajitas and freeze them in portions for easy use.

Day	Breakfast	Snack	Lunch	Snack	Dinner
Monday	Scrambled eggs with bacon or smoked salmon on rye	Protein yoghurt with fruit, nuts and honey	Cottage cheese and roast chicken wraps; lunchboxes for the kids	Tuna on rice cakes; potato sticks for the kids	Minced beef nachos with beans, avocado and salad
Tuesday	Hard-boiled eggs; cheese and ham toasties for the kids	Leftovers	Ham and slaw rolls; lunchboxes for the kids	Savoury cheese, ham and spinach muffins (airfryer)	Camp lamb burger (see page 136)
Wednesday	Warm bread and spreads	Hummus and veggies	Spinach quiche; lunchboxes for the kids	Cheese plate with dried fruits and crackers	Mushroom and chicken carbonara
Thursday	Porridge with blueberries	Banana bread or leftover quiche	Potato whitebait cakes (see page 204); lunchboxes for the kids	Rice paper rolls with leftovers	BBQ lamb koftas with Greek salad
Friday	Salmon frittata	Fresh fruit	Leftovers in tacos	Yoghurt and nuts	Broccoli salad and steak with sweet potato mash
Saturday	Pancakes with fruit	Cheese platter	Chicken Caesar wraps	Fresh fruits	Karaage chicken ciabatta burger (see page 242)
Sunday	Breakfast tacos	Road-trip bounty balls (see page 288)	Chicken salad sandwich	Cheese and crackers	Chicken tikka with flatbread
Monday	Cottage cheese on toast	Boiled eggs with mini cucumbers	Vietnamese noodle salad	Mini sausage rolls	Lemon zucchini salad with pan-seared chicken
Tuesday	Breakfast wrap	Carrots and hummus	Leftovers in a sandwich	Raw fish (see page 92) with corn chips	Meatballs
Wednesday	Shakshuka eggs with leftovers from meatballs	Road-trip bounty balls (see page 288) and green tea	Teriyaki chicken on rice with veggies	Rice cakes with peanut butter	Fish tacos (see page 104) with guacamole and corn chips
Thursday	Omelette	Bruschetta	Chicken quesadilla with avocado	Muffins	Minced chicken san choy bao
Friday	Cottage cheese and tomatoes on rye	Banana and peanut butter on rice cakes and cheese on Vita-Weats	Hot toasties with Peanut-butter brownie (see page 196)	Boiled eggs and trail mix	Green-lipped mussels in red sauce (see page 190)
Saturday	Breakfast muffins	Leftovers	Use up fridge day	Veggie plate	Chicken fajitas
Sunday	Breakfast bagels	Peanut-butter brownie (see page 196)	Vermicelli noodles in a jar with leftovers	Trail mix	Steak sandwich

Clothes and personal items

For over a decade, I have been using packing cubes to organise my travel clothing. They are the ultimate space-savers, allowing you to fit more into your suitcase without feeling overwhelmed. My first purchase, online from Amazon, has proved to be incredibly durable and has lasted our family years. As my family has grown, so has my collection. I have even colour-coordinated each set to help my family stay organised.

Here is an example of what I would pack for each person:

Adults

4 x T-shirts (or 4 x dresses, or a combination)
2 x shorts
2 x pajamas
2 x long-sleeve shirts
2 x long pants/jeans
2 x jumpers/sweatshirts
7 x underwear
7 x pairs of socks
2 x swimming togs/swim shorts
2 x jackets (1 rain and 1 winter)
water bottle
backpack

Kids

6 x T-shirts (or a mix of shirts and dresses)
4 x shorts, skirts and leggings
2 x pajamas
2 x long pants
4 x jumpers (New Zealand's climate really called for warm pullovers!)
7 x underwear
2 x jackets (1 rain and 1 winter)
water bottle
backpack

Baby

4 x sleepsuits
7 x singlets
5 x sets pants and tops
4 x socks
5 x jumpers
2 x jackets (1 rain and 1 winter)
ErgoPouch portable bassinet (newborn to 6 months) or Phil&Teds travel cot
travel pram/carrier
foldable bath (I used a Stokke Flexi Bath)

Tips

- Have a pair of comfortable jandals for daily use, especially for walks, although my children prefer to just wear slides.
- I use vacuum bags with my 12-volt vacuum to pack down anything we aren't actively using. I also have woven baskets of different sizes to store books, towels, linens and bulky clothing.
- When packing for kids, remember they will outgrow their clothes. They are also likely to need more seasonal clothes.
- My go-to camping hack is to put a scoop of Vanish into a large zip lock bag. Whenever someone gets a stain on their clothes, I put the item in the bag, add some water, shake it and leave it to soak until it's ready to be washed. I also carry a few pre-made packs in the boot.

Being prepared

You never know what might happen on the road, so it can be helpful to do some pre-planning for unexpected situations. Whether you have hired a van or are in your own vehicle, breakdowns happen. I can't begin to count the number of times we have broken down over the last five years.

What I have learned is to embrace the breakdowns. Some of the most magical experiences or people we have met that we would otherwise have missed have been because we have been stuck somewhere, waiting for parts. So the next time you encounter an unexpected breakdown, don't stress about it — take it in your stride and realise it's all part of the journey. You never know — the experience you have might turn out to be one of the highlights of your trip!

Take some time before you hit the road to learn about your vehicle. Before setting off, we learned a lot about Kombi maintenance and the problems we might encounter on the road. This meant we had a fair idea of anything that could happen and how to diagnose it, and were even able to make quick roadside repairs without calling for help.

Here are some useful tips for being prepared:

- Get good roadside/breakdown assistance. We have always opted for the top level of cover when travelling around both Australia and New Zealand. This type of cover usually includes towing and accommodation costs, and rental cars if needed. We have found it to be worth every penny, and it has taken a lot of the stress out of each situation. In New Zealand, we use the AA and have found them to be extremely helpful and easy to deal with.
- Make sure you have adequate insurance. Car and caravan insurance is vital, especially when you are living in your home on wheels. The New Zealand Motor Caravan Association offers specialist RV and caravan insurance.
- Carry tools and spare parts. Lockie does all of our maintenance; he is completely self-taught and has learned a lot about our VW after numerous breakdowns! It's hard to determine a definitive list of tools and parts you might need as each vehicle is different, and as you get to know your vehicle better, you will begin to fine-tune what you need to carry. For us, typically the same things go wrong multiple times, so we carry spares for:
  - clutch and accelerator cables
  - spark plugs
  - belts
  - fuses.

Depending on your vehicle, a general list of tools and supplies should include:
- oil
- WD-40 lubricant
- degreaser and brake cleaner
- coolant (for water-cooled vehicles)
- brake fluid
- a good jack — we carry a bottle jack as they are small and can lift very high
- wheel brace
- axle stands (if you plan to do your own maintenance)
- socket and spanner set
- jumper leads or battery jump-starter
- spare fuses
- Phillips and flathead screwdrivers
- Allen keys and star/Torx keys
- a multimeter is great for checking electrical currents on either the car, van or caravan
- a timing light, depending on how far you want to go with servicing.

I picked up a black storage tub from Mitre 10 to neatly store everything and keep the oily stuff safely away from staining anything. We also have a good VW parts specialist contact, who sends anything we need quickly, wherever we are.

- Carry out preventative maintenance. There aren't many mornings that I don't see Lockie looking in our engine bay or under the van, checking everything before we head off. Thoroughly inspect your vehicle before embarking on a trip and fix anything that looks like it might become a problem. We have found being proactive is beneficial. When on the road, regularly check the engine oil and use the best-quality fuel. Preventative maintenance is especially important when travelling during the winter months or in bad weather, when a breakdown could cause serious problems.
- Check your tyres, including the spare. We all understand the importance of having a good amount of tread, especially when towing. The roads in New Zealand can be tough on tyres (and brakes) due to the varied terrain, so it is essential to check your tyres regularly, especially before embarking on a long drive.
- Have enough food and water aboard. Always carry food and water with you, as I have learned through many breakdowns that repairs can take a few hours. Most of the time, we have been pretty close to a town, but having adequate food and water close at hand is essential in case of unexpected delays.
- Rust prevention is vital. Travelling in an old vehicle has lots of challenges, and one of the biggest ones is rust. There are so many incredible sites close to salt water, but the by-product is the potential for corrosion. We try our best to wash Izzie around every

three days to remove any salt. Lockie then goes around with a rust spray called Penetrol; this spray flows easily into small crevices and drives out air and moisture, taking away the 'food' rust needs to grow and literally stopping any rust in its tracks. Over the years, we have tried many other products but have had the greatest success with this.
- Fuel up your vehicle before starting any long journey, especially if you are driving an older vehicle like ours with a temperamental fuel gauge. Better to be safe than sorry!
- It is a great idea to complete a first-aid course through organisations such as Red Cross or St John, especially if you are travelling with children. They will also give you good advice on what to include in your first-aid kit. Fortunately, in New Zealand you don't have to worry about snakes — phew!

Budgeting

Planning a van trip can be an exciting time, but budgeting is part of the process that can be less enjoyable. Whether taking a short trip or living in your van permanently, knowing how much money you have to spend and keeping an eye on expenses is crucial, especially if you want to include more paid activities in your itinerary. By taking a proactive approach to budget planning, you can ensure a memorable trip without any financial worries.

Expenses on the road can differ significantly from person to person and family to family. Set a goal, create a list of the paid activities you wish to do during your trip and then research their costs. This not only helps you estimate your expenses but also make decisions about what it is worth spending your money on.

As well as making sure you have enough money to cover your day-to-day expenses, it's also vital to have some savings tucked away for any unforeseen emergencies, such as mechanical issues. You don't want your trip to come to a halt or to be stuck somewhere for an extended period because you can't afford repairs.

A budget and savings calculator app can be an excellent tool to help you keep track of your finances. I use Wanderlog, which includes a road-trip toggle with routing and currency exchange functions. Tripcoin is another fantastic app to consider, as it's free and straightforward to use, but it is only available for iOS.

On our first lap of Australia we were working and travelling on our weeks off. During our work commitments we stored the Kombi and flew back to Japan. Through our full-time Covid trip we used a massive chunk of our personal savings, then after some time on the road we began to make money from social media and photography. Following is a rough indication of our spending.

Groceries

I like to make bulk meals and freeze them, although our freezer space is limited. We tend to do two grocery shops a week, with each one lasting us for three or four days. Our grocery budget is usually around $350–$450 per week, for two adults and three children.

We enjoy trying out local food and supporting local suppliers wherever we can. We like to visit fresh food markets, roadside stalls and cute cafés. Sometimes we spend a bit extra on food just to treat ourselves and the kids to something like sushi.

Caravan parks

Fees vary depending on the location and the ages of your children. Some parks charge for kids from three years old, while others don't charge for small children at all. Additionally, waterfront spots can cost an extra $15 per night. To save money, consider booking sites back from the beach — they are often lovely and quiet as well.

On average, we found that the cost for a site that accommodated our setup and three children, with a loyalty discount, was around $65 per night.

Department of Conservation (DOC) campsites (see page 46 for more information on these) are an economical option.

Activities

In New Zealand I used the GrabOne website (www.new.grabone.co.nz) to save money on experiences. It updates daily, with great local deals including many fun activities from 25 to 50 per cent off.

We can spend around $500 a month on activities, bearing in mind that some weeks we don't spend anything at all or not everyone might do an activity; for example, only Riley wanted to do the Hydro Attack shark ride in Queenstown.

Fuel

We spend a lot on fuel, as high octane is our preferred choice. We are towing a caravan behind our Kombi, and although it is lightweight it increases our fuel consumption, especially on hills. We usually get around 350–400 km per tank, and while fuel prices vary throughout New Zealand, a full tank usually costs us between $140–$160.

Fuel is a significant expense on any road trip, but saving money on this essential commodity can be challenging. Woolworths supermarkets and BP fuel stations are partnered on a rewards programme, and Z Energy is partnered with New World and PAK'nSAVE. Flybuys and Air New Zealand's Airpoints programmes also offer fuel discounts. Z Sharetank is a brilliant little fuel hack — you can prepay for your fuel while the prices are low by topping up your Z account.

Tip

If you're travelling through small towns, note that fuel prices can be significantly higher there than in main centres. To avoid paying more than you need to, fuel up in the main towns before continuing your journey, and keep an eye on prices with the Gaspy app (see page 54).

Sample budget

Food	$350–$450 per week
Caravan parks	$65–$85 per night, $455–$595 per week
Activities	$125 per week
Fuel	$150 per week
Total	$1080–$1320 per week

Loyalty programmes

Consider joining caravan-park loyalty programmes to save money and get discounts on activities and other tourism operators. Look out for Tasman Holiday Parks for discounts on activities and the Interislander ferry. TOP 10 Holiday Parks offer a discount on each stay once you have joined their loyalty membership.

Other discounts

NZMCA membership offers many discounts on ferries, parks, activities and camping stores. The discounts on fuel are particularly handy for road-tripping.

By planning ahead, doing some research and looking for deals and discounts, you can make your trip more affordable and enjoyable. To save money on activities, check out the deals online such as the early-bird dining offer by First Table (www.firsttable.co.nz), available at numerous restaurants across New Zealand. By dining early, you can take advantage of a 50 per cent discount on your meal. Some activity operators also offer a discount for the first ride of the day — there's no harm in asking!

Finding work while travelling

Even if you've done the hard yards and saved up heaps of money to pay for your trip, you might find it useful to earn some extra money on the road. Here are some ideas.

Digital work

The online world offers many opportunities, including building websites, tutoring, editing, videography and more. Lots of travellers like ourselves use external professionals — we have a teacher for Riley, and a digital fitness programme — so consider if you have a skill that you can turn into a business on the road.

Social media

There are various options available for working on social media. Many companies are looking for employees to format and work as social-media strategists for their businesses. Additionally, sharing your own work, from fitness to travel, on your own social platform can help you earn money.

Photography

Are you an avid photographer? Could you capture your experiences and stunning landscapes, and sell your images digitally or to tourism boards? In our years of travel, this has been our best source of income. Many of our images have been purchased and featured in newspapers, magazines and billboards.

Stop-and-start work

Depending on your skills, you might be able to find temporary or casual work along the way. Opportunities for nurses, builders, cleaners, hotel staff, landscapers and café workers pop up in almost every town. These jobs often pay well and are a great way to meet new people. There is also often seasonal work available: fruit picking, ski instruction, tourism staff and farming/vineyard work.

If you plan to work during your travels and stay in one place for a while, I recommend starting with community Facebook forums. These forums usually have plenty of seasonal work listed.

Camping life

New Zealand is an ideal destination for nature enthusiasts who want to embark on an adventure. You can experience camping amidst the soothing sounds of birdsong in the bush or waves crashing against beach pebbles. The country is proud of its natural beauty and, as a result, offers a range of camping options that maximise and preserve it.

The diverse range of camping options throughout New Zealand is one of its major attractions. With an abundance of waterfront caravan parks, over 500 free camps and hundreds of Department of Conservation (DOC) camps, it really does cater for everyone. We like to mix it up and use all three regularly. This journey is about all of us and although Lockie and I love a freedom camp with lots of solitude, it's not always the most fun for the kids. Caravan parks with playgrounds and other friends to play with is what they absolutely love, so we ensure we stay there regularly so everyone's cup is full. Caravan parks are also wonderful if you are in need of facilities such as power and bathrooms but still want to feel disconnected from the mainstream and live in nature.

Another option is staying in DOC campsites in national parks and other natural areas. These sites are cheap and many have toilet facilities and water. The last option is freedom camping on public reserves. It is an incredible privilege to be able to camp for free in many stunning locations. I implore you to please be respectful, take your rubbish with you and always ensure you leave the camp exactly as you found it.

Camp etiquette

We always strive to find exceptional camping experiences, but we make sure to be courteous campers. Whether we stay at wilderness sites or commercial campgrounds, we ensure that we leave no trace. This means that we pack up all rubbish and dispose of it in the provided bins or take it to the nearest facility if no bins are available.

We take extra care to avoid damaging the natural surroundings by using designated trails and following established camping guidelines. Our commitment to leaving the environment pristine is a top priority, and we take great pride in being responsible while enjoying the great outdoors.

We also make sure to space ourselves appropriately, giving other campers enough room. We appreciate the sounds of waves and birds, but we understand that our caravans and vans don't have sound insulation. Therefore, we keep the noise levels to a minimum after 10 p.m.

When driving in camping areas, we drive slowly since children often play nearby. We take our time in open sites to

ensure the safety of anyone in the area.

Rubbish and recycling bins and waste dump stations are available at various locations nationwide, especially in popular camping areas. NZMCA has a list of dump stations on its website but we have found Google works well for finding dump stations in the area we are in. These stations are free to use and provide a convenient disposal method.

If you are not at a commercial caravan park, household rubbish can be disposed of at council waste stations and refuse centres. Prices vary from town to town. KiwiCash sites also offer recycling (see page 54).

Finding a place to camp

The WikiCamps app is a large database of campgrounds, caravan parks and other facilities. The DOC website is the source of information for park camping, and is frequently updated with the latest on access, closures and other useful information.

Designated areas for freedom camping vary around the country. Many are well sign-posted, either welcoming you to their spot or specifying where camping is forbidden. Council-controlled freedom camping locations generally have facilities such as toilets nearby.

Department of Conservation campsites

DOC runs campsites around the country, divided into tiers with various levels of facilities. These campsites provide access to New Zealand's national parks and other areas of stunning natural scenery. Check their website for maps and booking information (www.doc.govt.nz).

Serviced campsites

Serviced campsites offer amenities such as flush toilets, treated/untreated tap water, cooking benches, hot showers and rubbish collection. Remember to boil untreated water before drinking. Many serviced campsites also offer additional amenities such as laundry, barbecues, fireplaces, cookers and picnic tables.

Standard campsites

Expect basic amenities such as toilets, vehicle or boat access, and untreated tap water or other sources of water. In order to maintain cleanliness and health, campers must bring their own soap for hand washing. It is also essential to boil any untreated water supply before use or consumption to ensure safety. Some campsites may offer additional facilities such as cold showers, wood barbecues and fireplaces, picnic tables, a cooking shelter and rubbish bins. The range of available facilities and services varies, so check beforehand what a particular campsite offers.

Basic campsites

Camping at a basic site is a great way to enjoy nature, but this free option does, however, come with the responsibility of being self-sufficient. Some sites may have limited facilities, and it's recommended to boil untreated water before use.

DOC Campsite Pass

A 30- or 365-night Campsite Pass gives you access to DOC campsites all around New Zealand, some of which can be booked on the DOC website or at a DOC visitor centre. Having a Campsite Pass is not a guarantee of a site, and booking may be required, along with registration of arrival.

Campfires

As you read through this book, you'll notice our fondness for campfires. Gazing into the flames under the night sky is all part of the atmosphere, isn't it? However, to ensure that you enjoy your toasted marshmallows safely, there are a few golden rules for building a campfire.

Firstly, before lighting any outdoor fire, you should check whether you need a fire permit from Fire and Emergency NZ, depending on the fire season. Go to www.checkitsalright.nz and enter the details of what kind of fire you want to light, where and when. Additionally, it's vital to check local council rules and bylaws since there may be regulations regarding lighting fires in your camping area.

You should also check the weather forecast before lighting your campfire, and only do it on days when the fire danger is low and the wind is not too strong.

When you're setting up and lighting your campfire, choose a location away from anything flammable, such as tents, vehicles, overhanging branches, dry vegetation, buildings, fences and other items that could catch fire. Clear a 3-metre space around the fire and keep it away from any property boundaries. If you're staying at a hut or campground, use the designated cooking areas for your campfire.

To prevent your campfire from getting out of control, keep it small, less than half-a-metre high and wide, and burn only clean, dry, untreated wood. Add small amounts at a time, and keep a bucket of water or fire extinguisher nearby. Never leave it unattended, and make sure at least one person is constantly monitoring your campfire.

Finally, when you're ready to put out your campfire, douse it with lots of water. Once it's drowned, check it's completely out and mix the ashes and embers with soil or sand.

By following these safety measures, you can enjoy your campfire responsibly while minimising the risk of starting a wildfire and protecting our environment.

Travelling with kids

Travelling with children can be a rewarding experience, creating lasting memories and helping the kids develop into well-rounded individuals. Interacting with other kids from different cultures, trying new foods and learning about history can be highly beneficial, and is something we value for our children.

Before we began our Kombi adventures, we lived in Tokyo and used it as a base for exploring numerous countries. By the time our son Riley was one year old, he had already visited 37 countries! We soon discovered that children can make excellent travel companions and this was our stepping stone to camping with kids.

We are now a family with three children, aged one to seven. Riley and his sister Alba have learned how to pack their backpacks, navigate with a map, eat breakfast with sandy toes and share a tiny caravan, and baby Elsie is learning those same skills. We have also learnt so much during our seven years of travelling with kids, from avoiding overpacking to hiking tips and how to entertain kids on long Kombi drives.

Safety is our top priority, so we always ensure that all three children are securely fastened in good car-seats. Due to the age of our van, we needed to modify it to install anchor points for each seat. We chose Britax seats because of their excellent safety rating and comfort, which is essential when taking long drives.

Personal belongings

We aren't big into material things; we often celebrate birthdays together enjoying our favourite food and a fun day doing something we love instead of giving gifts. However, it is nice for the kids to have some treasures. We exchange many books with other families at caravan parks during our travels, and pass them on to others. We also like to pick up games and toys from second-hand shops to keep things interesting. A bucket with outdoor games lives in our boot — sports balls, jump ropes, boogie boards and chalk for hopscotch — and inside, we have games like Bananagrams, Snakes and Ladders and UNO, which are fun ways to pass the time. My kids love Lego, too — it is an excellent box of quiet fun for those rainy days.

Anything we love but no longer use we box up and post to our storage unit, especially the baby items that we no longer require. Salvation Army family stores are a wonderful place to pass items onto, or if you're after some extra cash, sell your goods on Facebook Marketplace.

Schooling

Homeschooling can be scary, especially when travelling, but we've found ways to make it work for Riley. Finding the right programme for your family is the best place to start.

We experimented with different methods since Riley began school, beginning with the Australian distance education system, which was a great starting point. Everything was pre-recorded online, with printable worksheets and examinations. Now that we're in New Zealand, we have switched to Euka, an online homeschooling programme that regularly sends content to us. We also carry a tub of books and educational activities for Riley. All the resources are sent out or are online.

With Euka's online planner, we work out a daily routine for Riley's learning. This includes bookwork and maths, followed by outdoor learning, geography and history later in the day. We end the day with word and number quizzes. I organise each subject into folders to keep things stress-free. On slower days, we utilise tools like Reading Eggs, or worksheets from Euka and Kmart booklets.

Keeping a diary is essential to track Riley's progress and any challenges he might face. We can easily talk with Euka about any queries. Regular progress reports are sent to us, and we also self-evaluate and make any necessary changes to fit Riley's learning style. We have learned a lot about Riley through this journey, and can tailor the programme to fit his learning level and interests. We often use marine life and dinosaurs, which Riley loves, as tools for different activities.

There are days when Riley finishes everything in two hours, while on other days it takes him more time. There are days we miss things, but due to our lifestyle, we can easily catch up. The flexibility of this form of learning allows us to adjust to Riley's pace. We have noticed that Riley learns better and is more successful when he is happy and relaxed.

Reading Eggs has been a great learning tool for both Riley and Alba. It tracks their learning abilities and highlights their strengths and weaknesses. When Elsie was born, and during the caravan renovation and newborn phase, we hired an online tutor for reading via Zoom, and Riley responded so well. This was an excellent resource for scenarios like ours.

'Worldschooling'

While we are out and about, we work together learning about places and their culture and history. Exploring together as a family is a great way to bond, and to help children learn their limits and boundaries.

We select treks and hikes suitable for our children's ages and how they feel on the day. We always pack lightweight snacks, as they are a source of encouragement for our family. In warmer destinations, we treat ourselves to ice-block tubes stored in a Thermos for a refreshing cool-down. We pack lightweight towels in case there's a place for a swim, and each person has a water bottle with a handle for easy carrying. Before leaving, we brief the kids on the difficulty level and time of the walk, and provide them with a map so they can navigate easily.

When planning our travels, we like to involve our kids in the process. We discuss new destinations with them and ask about their interests and what they want to do there. We make the kids maps using Google Maps: we print out an area and the kids can put stickers on them and write what they like. This helps them visualise where we are going and have conversations about each destination's unique aspects. We prioritise and plan accordingly, to ensure a fun trip for the whole family.

Social interaction

Ever since Riley was born, he has had a happy and confident personality, and he is naturally skilled at socialising with other children. Whether we are at playgrounds, caravan parks or the beach, he never hesitates to introduce himself to other kids and join in on their games. It's a delight to see Riley immerse himself in playtime. He has also been an excellent role model for Alba, who finds it easy to socialise with other children as well.

However, what we found especially remarkable is the bond Riley shares with his siblings. They play together with ease and joy, and it's inspiring to see how they always include each other in group activities.

Travelling with babies

Babies can make great little travel companions. We have travelled with all three children from an early age. They were all breastfed on demand, which made it easier for us as I didn't have to worry about bottles and keeping milk. Fortunately, they all slept very well through the night from a reasonable age, which made my life very manageable.

When Elsie was six weeks old, we moved into the caravan, and started using a Phil&Teds travel cot for her to sleep in. It is easy to assemble, folds away quickly and is also a great play-pen for outside.

On the road the kids quickly fell into a natural rhythm of sleep routines, eating and play, without too much restriction. I have always trusted my intuition and gut feeling, so when it comes to life on the road with three kids I have never felt too overwhelmed and everyone has been able to live pretty normal lives.

When travelling with a baby, there are a few essential items that can make the journey much easier. Our top priority is a safe car-seat, and we opted for the Britax Millenia, which has a five-star rating and excellent support from newborn to six years old. Elsie loves napping in it during our morning drives. We also recommend the foldable Stokke Flexi Bath, which is durable and can double as a washing basket. A lightweight pram is helpful for trips to the grocery store or camp showers. During Elsie's infant stage, we used a bassinet-style pram that she loved sleeping in.

To keep all of the baby's things organised, we use a caddy for nappies, wipes, creams, first-aid supplies and clothes. Even if your child doesn't use bottles, carrying drink bottles and soft silicone plates and cutlery while travelling is always handy.

As Elsie grew older, we began using a Max & Koko mini camping highchair, so she could be included in meal times.

A suitable baby carrier is also vital for short walks, hikes, and generally getting around. It protects your back and keeps your baby comfortable while you bond with them. We've tried brands such as Ergobaby, Redsbaby and Chekoh.

Lastly, for playtime, we have a subscription to an age-appropriate, stage-based learning and play kit that is sent out every three months to help Elsie develop her motor skills and enjoy playtime.

Must-have apps

Thanks to advances in technology, there are now some great apps that can enhance your road trip experience. These can help you plan your route, locate the best fuel prices, discover exciting places to stop along the way, and even help you find a place to stay for the night.

Wifi service and phones
We heavily depend on the internet for a lot of things, such as homeschooling, remote work and staying in touch with our family. To cater to our data needs, we use Spark SIM cards that allow us to stream, work online and make calls.

For communication, we usually rely on FaceTime to chat with our friends and family. We don't have a TV, but we have Netflix on devices so we can watch our favourite shows and movies.

The internet is also helpful for finding parking spots, campsites and laundromats, and getting directions. With options like Starlink satellite internet, staying connected while on the road is no longer a hassle.

Tip
One NZ offers a three-month SIM card with unlimited data and calls, available at the airport for around NZ $130. This is a great short-term option.

Google Maps
One of the most essential apps for any road trip. It's a reliable and user-friendly navigation app that provides real-time traffic updates, directions to your destination and alternative routes. With features like the ability to save location pins and access maps offline, plus voice-guided navigation, it'll help you stay on track.

Café Finder by Allpress
As travellers and parents, we rely on coffee to keep us going. We're always on the lookout for Allpress in particular, and I'm proud to say that it's Kiwi-made. We even met the creator on Waiheke Island, learning more about the man who powers our day. The Allpress app easily pinpoints cafés that serve their coffee, making it easy for us to get our fix on the go.

Gaspy
Use this to help you find the cheapest fuel in your area. This app can really help you save money on gas and keep your road trip budget in check.

KiwiCash
A convenient booking and payment system that provides access to designated campsites and facilities across New Zealand. It is accepted by selected DOC campsites, too. With KiwiCash, you can top up your personal balance for the facilities you need, including drive-in

facilities, laundry, dishwashing, power points, toilets and showers. These campsites are open to all travellers, regardless of the type of vehicle or camping style, and they are located throughout New Zealand.

Z App
Z App is pretty clever! Use your pre-set details to pay for fuel using your number plate, stack your Pumped discounts, and pay with Sharetank. Sharetank allows you to pre-buy fuel at the best price, search prices in a 30 km radius and use the fuel at that price when you are ready.

AA Roadservice
Join the New Zealand AA for roadside assistance 24/7, as well as other member discounts.

WikiCamps New Zealand and CamperMate
These apps provide helpful information on campsites, holiday parks and other accommodation options across New Zealand.

MetService and Windy.com
New Zealand's weather can be highly changeable. To make the most of your trip and stay safe, it's important to plan ahead and stay informed about the weather. Luckily, these two helpful apps can provide you with up-to-date weather forecasts and alerts, so you can adjust your plans accordingly.

Instagram
Using the location toggle, discover many beautiful sunset locations, hikes and visual guides to this impressive country. Don't forget to say hello to us over at @theslowroad_.

Tripcoin
This travel-budget planning app is designed to help you manage your finances on the road. With daily graphs and real-time conversion rates, you can keep track of your spending and plan your budget accordingly.

Roady
This app can help you discover exciting attractions, scenic routes and hidden gems along the way, drawing on the advice of expert travellers.

ON THE ROAD

NORTH ISLAND

Northland/Te Tai Tokerau

The Northland region of New Zealand, stretching upwards from Auckland, boasts a subtropical climate and stunning natural landscapes. Taking a road trip along the Twin Coast Discovery Highway is the best way to take in all its beauty. On the east coast, there are breathtaking views of the Bay of Islands and its collection of more than 140 islands renowned for their pristine beaches and abundant marine life. On the western side lies the Kauri Coast and the forests which are home to the world's largest kauri trees, which can grow up to 50 metres tall and live for over 2000 years. The Far North is a rugged and remote region known for its stunning beaches, crystal-clear waters, and untouched wilderness.

Mangawhai

This slice of paradise a little more than an hour north of Auckland isn't one to miss! There is lots for water lovers to enjoy, from fishing to kite surfing.

Explore
The Mangawhai Cliffs walkway is a beloved local walk that is great for families, with fantastic ocean views along the way.

Eat
Wood Street Pizzeria offers a relaxing atmosphere for enjoying a decent meal after a long drive. Everyone was happy with the pizza, especially the pork belly and BBQ sauce.

Camp
Mangawhai Heads Holiday Park: In a prime location right on the estuary, with views of the sandspit.

Waipu

Located on Bream Bay, the lovely township of Waipu is situated on a gorgeous white-sand beach that's great for safe swimming, surfing and fishing. Kids will enjoy exploring the rock pools and secluded areas. Horse riding is also a popular activity on the beach at Waipu, and further north at Uretiti and Ruakākā. Head to the main town of Waipu for groceries and anything else you need.

We enjoyed a day at Langs Beach, just south of Waipu, before heading to dinner at The Cove, which is a picturesque spot for a meal. Check out the museum, art gallery and — my favourite — the vintage store in the township, to find some treasures.

Explore
For nature enthusiasts, the Waipu Caves are a great exploration. It's a 1.5-hour round trip to discover beautiful stalactites, stalagmites and glowworms. Make sure to wear sturdy shoes (or preferably water shoes) as it can be slippery, and don't forget to bring a torch.

Explore the Waipu Coastal Walkway between Waipu Cove and Langs Beach, for breathtaking rock formations and beautiful sea views.

Piroa Falls in the Waipu Gorge Scenic Reserve is an easy track to a pretty waterfall.

Take in the fresh air and slow the day down with a walk along Langs Beach and McKenzie Cove.

Experience
Drop in to Marsden Cove Marina and check out charter tours that include fishing, diving and sightseeing on Bream Bay and around Whangārei Heads.

Learn 2 Surf Waipu Cove is a great way for the kids to give surfing a go.

Eat
McLeod's Pizza Barn & Brewery was recommended to us and it definitely lived up to its reputation. The craft beer

was excellent and went well with the tasty pizza.

The Bach Cafe at Ruakākā Beach, further north, is a great spot to enjoy some good coffee and breakfast. Soak up the warm sun while chatting with some friendly locals.

Camp
Camp Waipu Cove: Sitting pretty back from the beach with all the creature comforts of a campground.

Uretiti Beach DOC campsite: Coin-operated hot shower and hosts on-site year round.

Whangārei

The city of Whangārei offers a blend of urban and natural attractions, with a vibrant arts and culture scene, stunning parks and gardens, and easy access to some of the region's most beautiful beaches and coastal walking trails.

Explore
Mount Manaia is situated above McLeod Bay at Whangārei Heads. The track is 2 hours return and is such a stunning spot to watch the sunset — you may even spot a kiwi in the wild. Great for older children, as it is a fair way for smaller children.

Enjoy Whangārei Falls for a fun day out. View the falls from above on the viewing platform or enjoy the soothing sounds of the water from below after a short 10-minute walk.

Northland's only kiwi house is at Kiwi North, a complex which also includes the Whangārei Museum and Heritage Park. Next door is the Whangarei Native Bird Recovery Centre, where injured birds are rehabilitated before they are released back into the wild.

Tutukaka

On the coast north of Whangārei are Tutukaka and Matapouri, both showcasing beautiful, clear, blue bays.

Explore
Dive! Tutukaka is a locally run business that will take you on an extraordinary trip to discover marine life and dive around the subtropical Poor Knights Islands.

Ngunguru is a wonderful place to stop and stretch the legs, with lots of outdoor fun to enjoy, from kayaking to bush walks.

The Taiharuru River estuary is a complete glass-off each morning — perfect for a morning stand-up paddleboard.

Whale Bay at Matapouri has rock pools to splash in, and safe swimming at the estuary, river or beach. Locals recommend fishing from the rocks.

Camp
Tutukaka Holiday Park: A classic Kiwi holiday park, lush with greenery. Located next to the Tutukaka Marina.

Bay of Islands

Seeking crystal-clear, turquoise waters and soft sandy beaches? Well, here they are. Once you discover the serene beauty of the Bay of Islands you will understand why marine life — and holidaymakers — love it. From the historic lodge at Otehei Bay to the vibrant atmosphere of Kerikeri, this area is stunning.

This is an area of immense historic significance: Waitangi witnessed the drafting and signing of the treaty which bears its name. It's a great place to learn about Māori culture and the significant events associated with the signing of the treaty. Visit the Waitangi Treaty Grounds and see the carved meeting house, one of the largest Māori canoes in the country and two museums, Te Kōngahu and Te Rau Aroha, as well as witnessing a stunning cultural performance. I particularly enjoyed the Māori Battalion exhibit, which features a large portrait of my grandfather's brother, Pirimia Te Kani.

Paihia/Russell

Enjoy stunning views of the bay where warriors, whalers, sailors and settlers once lived side by side.

Explore
As you drive alongside the glistening waters to enter the township of Paihia, there is an undoubtedly instinctive pull to the water. Enjoy a dip in the warm, shallow waters at Paihia Beach or Te Tii, towards Waitangi.

Take a peaceful walk through bush and a mangrove forest to Haruru Falls.

Experience
There is an array of local operators in Paihia, offering a wonderful selection of scenic experiences. See the Bay from above with a helicopter tour, or take a day cruise to the Hole in the Rock, spotting dolphins along the way.

Island-hop around Urupukapuka Island and take in the bluest water at Otehei Bay.

If you are feeling wild and the weather is pristine, go for a parasail with Flying Kiwi Parasail.

Take a ferry ride to Russell, or Kororāreka as it was known when it was the first capital of New Zealand. This charming little town has beautiful souvenir shops and clothing shops, such as Caravan Clothing & Home, for a browse. Don't forget to try some oysters at the waterfront Duke of Marlborough Hotel, renowned for being the first establishment in the country to receive an official liquor licence.

Complete the day with a refreshing swim at Long Beach/Oneroa Bay, over the hill from the Russell township.

Eat

Enjoy beachside fish and chips at JFC in Paihia. This colonial building might make you feel like you are stepping into a fancy hotel, but it's home to the most delicious Kiwi-style fish and chips.

The Tipsy Oyster in Paihia township is a fun and vibrant place to spend the evening over a dozen oysters prepared in interesting ways.

Hone's Garden in Russell offers a fun and chill atmosphere, good craft beer, great food and cool people.

Take the best seat in Russell and enjoy lunch at Omata Estate — their pizza is phenomenal and the location is unmatched, overlooking the water amongst the vines.

Camp

Waitangi Holiday Park: Sitting on the Waitangi River, you can enjoy views of the river.

Bay of Islands Holiday Park: Bushy, grassy spots with a river running through the grounds.

Paihia TOP 10 Holiday Park: Stunning ocean views and close to town.

Russell TOP 10 Holiday Park: Surrounded by a large grassy park and within easy walking distance of the township.

Kerikeri

About half an hour from Paihia lies the township of Kerikeri, which has a rich Māori and European history, including the planting of the first grapevines in New Zealand, in 1819 by missionary Samuel Marsden.

Experience

If you happen to visit Kerikeri on a market day (Friday nights, Saturdays or Sundays), you're in for a treat. The Old Packhouse building has now become a local community hub, where you can find lots of yummy local produce, bakers' delights and wonderful handmade arts and crafts.

Across the road, Keri Berries Farm Store awaits with their fresh berry ice cream, which is a must-try. Check out the deli-style store full of local goodies, great gifts and delicious treats.

Spend the afternoon getting up close to Rainbow Falls, an easy trek suitable for families.

Camp

Kerikeri Campground Wagon Wheel Holiday Park: An easy base for venturing. Treat yourself to the delicious local cafes a short stroll away.

Hidden gem

Charlie's Rock is a great swimming hole to enjoy on a hot day. Get there via the short walkway off Landing Road, Waipapa.

Matauri Bay

Matauri Bay is a picturesque and popular holiday destination located 30 km northeast of Kerikeri.

Camp
Matauri Bay Holiday Park: A cute and quiet spot to rest for the afternoon or overnight.

Tauranga Bay

After some quiet? This is the spot to rejuvenate. It is ideal for water activities; the little ones will enjoy boogie boarding and it is also great for rock fishing.

Camp
Tauranga Bay Holiday Park: An exquisite and unspoiled beachfront spot. You can relish the scenic beauty of the seaside while your kids have a great time in the park's vast open spaces. Take a stroll along the beach with your morning coffee and enjoy the breathtaking sunrise.

Taupō Bay

I had one of those moments where I spotted a sign and decided to drive in by chance. And to my surprise, it turned out to be an excellent stop. The bay was small, but filled with people enjoying the beach, and some even surfing the little waves. The kids were soon building sandcastles and taking dips in the water, while the baby slept soundly on the grassy bank. It's a place where life slows down, and you can simply enjoy a good book.

Camp
Taupō Bay Holiday Park: Plenty of space to spread out.

Mangōnui/Doubtless Bay

Doubtless Bay is a stunning bay located on the eastern coast of Northland, and is definitely worth a visit. There are several small settlements within the bay, which forms a horseshoe shape from Hihi and Mangōnui at the southeastern end to the Karikari Peninsula in the north.

Mangōnui is a beautiful area, which showcases some lovely historic buildings that can be explored by taking a walk along the heritage trail. Near this peaceful coastal town are some stunning beaches, complete with swaying palm trees. Stroll along the wharf to check out the fishing action.

Explore
The Rangikapiti Pā Historic Reserve provides a great viewpoint of the area. A short loop walk leads to the

Rangikapiti pā site, which has a rich history and is a significant cultural and historical landmark for the local community. As you walk along the trail, you will be able to admire the stunning views of Mangōnui Harbour and Doubtless Bay.

Eat
The Mangonui Fish Shop, situated near the Mangōnui wharf, has been voted as the best place for fish and chips in the North. After hearing so much about it, we decided to try it out for ourselves. We parked our Kombi and caravan at the nearest park and joined the long line of hungry patrons. Finally, we got our order of snapper with kūmara fries and fresh slices of Tip Top bread, which we took to Cable Bay to enjoy by the seaside. It was a delicious experience. We then went across the road to the Cable Bay Store to try their famous thickshakes — it was definitely worth it! Karikari's Salty Brew coffee caravan captured our eye, with its cute vintage caravan and yummy Allpress coffee.

Kids
Cable Bay is a fantastic spot for picnics and swimming, with plenty of rock pools to explore. Kids will also love Coopers Beach for kayaking and stand-up paddleboarding on the calm waters.

Camp
Hihi Beach Holiday Park: A genuine New Zealand holiday park, offering safe swimming, fishing and kayaking opportunities, and ample space to unwind. Loads of shelter and shade, as well as scope for kids to have fun and explore.

Freedom camp
Mill Bay and Mangonui Lions Park both offer back-to-basics camping. There is also a freedom camp at Tokerau Beach, on the western side of Doubtless Bay.

Kaitaia/Ahipara

Kaitaia boasts a rich cultural heritage. The area is known for its gumdigging history, and the local museum Te Ahu offers a fascinating insight into this industry, as well as the rich Māori heritage of the area.

For adventure-seekers and surf-lovers, Ahipara, at the southern end of Ninety Mile Beach, is a dream destination, home to curling waves — it has one of the best left-hand surf breaks in New Zealand — and seaside camping. Shipwreck Bay is a famous spot for surfers, and of course there are incredible sunsets over the sea.

Experience
Give Blokarting a go — it is a thrilling wind-powered activity for everyone. Ahipara Adventure Centre offers Blokart hire for all ages on Ninety Mile Beach, subject to wind conditions.

For an amazing experience for the entire family, take a ride along Ninety Mile Beach with Ahipara Horse Treks. I highly recommend going at sunset, for that extra glow.

Eat
Indian Spice Kaitaia: After a long drive to Cape Reinga and back (see below), a hot, fast and easy meal was needed. We were delighted by our meal from this restaurant and takeaway.

North Drift Cafe: I never go past a good coffee, and this cafe in Ahipara gave me my morning oomph. Great meals and a good selection of quick cabinet food, too.

Camp
Te Kōhanga Camping Ground: Located amidst native harakeke (flax) and bush, just a stone's throw from the beach. The campsite has a strong sense of community and provides a chance to listen to the birds while inhaling the fresh sea air.

Cape Reinga/Te Rerenga Wairua

Cape Reinga is a breathtaking coastal spot where the Tasman Sea and the Pacific Ocean meet. The Cape Reinga lighthouse is a remarkable historic landmark, located near the northernmost point of New Zealand. Situated atop a steep and rugged cliff, it offers spectacular views of where the oceans meet, as well as playing a crucial role in guiding ships around the top of the North Island. Take a leisurely stroll to the lighthouse, marvel at the stunning scenery, and discover the fascinating history and culture of the area.

This was on our family's bucket list, but it's a big drive: 95 km one way from Kaitaia. Make plenty of stops along the way to break the journey. Many people choose to stay in Kaitaia and make it a day trip, but there are other options to stay along the way.

Experience
Travelling to the top of the North Island is an exciting journey, with stunning stops on the way. We stopped at the famous sand dunes at Te Paki for an exhilarating, sandy ride.

Tip
If you don't have any, buy some cheap boogie boards from The Warehouse in Kaitaia before heading for the dunes, or you can hire them at the dunes.

Eat
Houhora Honey Bees: Don't let the name fool you — it's all about the pies. As well as traditional flavours like steak and cheese, there is a new contender in the pie game: pāua, known internationally as abalone. I had my first encounter with it at this fantastic roadside stop on the way up north.

Camp
Ngapae Holiday Park, Waipapakauri Ramp: A good base for tripping around Ninety Mile Beach.

Houhora Heads (Wagener) Holiday Park: An epic place to call home for a few days. Lots of wonderful facilities, right on the water.

Pukenui Holiday Park: A serene and family-friendly holiday park that is a favourite among travellers exploring the northernmost part of New Zealand.

Renowned for its excellent fishing opportunities and a comfortable, safe and welcoming environment.

Tapotupotu DOC campsite: Back-to-basics, this is the closest place to stay to Cape Reinga/Te Rerenga Wairua. Set up your campsite close to a beautiful lagoon that provides an ideal place to relax after some big walks.

Rarawa Beach DOC campsite: Camp next to Rarawa's white sandy beach. A lovely peaceful place to enjoy a good book.

Kauri Coast and Hokianga

West of the Bay of Islands lies the historic Hokianga Harbour. With lots to see and explore, this is a great place for lovers of nature and history.

Explore
Take a walk through the ancient Waipoua Forest and visit some of New Zealand's largest kauri, which have been standing tall for over 2000 years, including the grandaddy of them all, Tāne Mahuta.

Waiotemarama Falls are a stunning 15 minutes' drive inland from Opononi. The waterfall walk takes around 25 minutes with kids and leads to the waterfall's base.

Experience
Manea Footprints of Kupe: Learn about the intrepid adventures of Kupe in the Manea Theatre of Life and explore the Footprints of Kupe Interactive Gallery to learn more about the area's rich history.

Northland is known for sand-boarding, and the Hokianga has some of the most stunning dunes in New Zealand. Kids can boogie-board down the dunes and shoot right into the water. Hop on board with Hokianga Express Charters to cross the harbour to the dunes, or go on a harbour cruise.

Eat
I am always on the hunt for great fish and chips, and Opononi Beach Takeaways offers great crispy batter at old-school prices.

Camp
Koutu Mangeroa: A small fee gives you access to this lovely beachside camp near Opononi. Campers must be self-contained.

DOC Waipoua Visitor Centre and Campground: Loved for its open spaces and closeness to the kauri forest.

Wairere Boulders Nature Reserve and Campsite: Stay overnight at the boulders (an attraction in themselves) and experience the awakening of nocturnal creatures in the nature reserve and clear night skies, free from light pollution.

Kauri Coast TOP 10 Holiday Park: Nestled near the huge kauri forests at Trounson Kauri Park and Waipoua Forest, this campground is set on 2 hectares of lush parkland, surrounded by beautiful native bush and bordered by two rivers.

Auckland/Tāmaki Makaurau

Auckland is a city that caters to socialites, with its assortment of chic bars and upscale eateries. However, the city isn't all about glitz and glamour. It is home to several stunning regional parks, a lively waterfront and beaches that are perfect for surfers. A stone's throw away from the city, discover many wonderful locations for campers. The region stretches from the Kaipara Harbour in the north down through the southern part of the Northland Peninsula. It passes through the Waitākere Ranges, the Auckland isthmus and the low-lying land surrounding Manukau Harbour. It ends just a few kilometres away from the mouth of the Waikato River. This is a wonderful destination for camping enthusiasts to enjoy.

Auckland

Auckland, often known as the City of Sails, is a vibrant and fun city that has a lot to offer. I enjoyed living here for eight years, mainly because I was in my twenties and it was all about socialising! Auckland has many beautiful areas, and there are hidden gems to discover while exploring the city. The city is diverse and exciting, with a bustling harbour frequently full of sailboats, great grassy parks, a fantastic zoo that is a must-visit for families with children, and the Sky Tower, which offers a panoramic view of the region.

Explore

Auckland is a waterfront city full of beautiful places to visit, with parks scattered throughout it, for everyone to enjoy. For families, Maungakiekie/One Tree Hill is a great spot to picnic and enjoy the views. It's surrounded by Cornwall Park, a fun place for friendly touch-rugby games — and indulge in some fresh scones from the cafe.

Closer to town, Pukekawa/Auckland Domain offers panoramic views of the city, and Ōrākei Basin has a walking track that is particularly stunning at sunset.

Selwyn Reserve, which runs along the golden sands of Mission Bay beach, provides breathtaking views of the Waitematā Harbour. Well-established pōhutukawa trees offer much-needed shade on hot summer days, and kids can enjoy the lighthouse-inspired playground and let out some road-trip energy.

Discover the beauty and vibrancy of Takapuna, a beachside destination with a city rhythm, only 10 minutes from Auckland's CBD. It offers a relaxed beach atmosphere combined with great shops and restaurants. While you are on the North Shore, head down to Devonport and take a stroll around the Torpedo Bay Navy Museum.

Experience

As a homeschooling family, we love to explore interactive places with our kids. One of our favourites is MOTAT (Museum of Transport and Technology), where you can discover the history of transportation.

The Auckland Zoo is very close to MOTAT, on the other side of the beautiful Western Springs Park. Here you can see our beloved kiwi and some cool insects that are special to New Zealand, in Te Wao Nui — The Living Realm, which takes you on a journey through six regions of New Zealand, and features many native species.

For those who enjoy boats, the New Zealand Maritime Museum is a great place to learn about all things related to the ocean. You can also get out on the water with one of the many marine tours available, such as the Auckland Harbour sailing experience with Explore Group.

The Sky Tower, New Zealand's tallest building, provides a 360-degree view of Auckland.

For rugby lovers, the All Blacks Experience at SkyCity is a must-visit. On a rainy day, this is a great activity that the kids will enjoy.

Rangitoto Island, with its distinctive, symmetrical cone and superb location just off the coast, is a fantastic place for those who enjoy the outdoors. It's an easy and short — not to mention scenic — ferry ride from downtown Auckland. Take a hike up to the summit (approximately 1 hour each way) to enjoy the panoramic views. Guided sea-kayaking trips to the island are also available, including a night kayak, where you can watch the sunset from the summit before paddling back under the stars towards the glowing city lights.

Eat

Britomart is the place where Auckland meets Melbourne. If you're looking for a luxurious dining experience, then the downtown Britomart area is where you should head. It is bustling with life and offers excellent options for both eating and shopping. I am a huge fan of Cafe Hanoi, a Vietnamese restaurant serving delicious food. I highly recommend their crispy turmeric pancake.

The Viaduct and Wynyard Quarter are perfect areas for a stroll by the harbour, and offer some of Auckland's best restaurants to satisfy your taste buds. Dr Rudi's rooftop brewery is an ideal place to unwind, a trendy yet relaxed place that offers exciting food and good beer that you can enjoy all on the rooftop. Children are welcome — they have a good kids' menu. We're big fans of their hot wings, which come smothered in a moreish hot sauce. Additionally, it's an excellent spot to watch the boats in action in the Viaduct.

Best Ugly Bagels are so good that they almost feel like an indulgence! They are located 10 minutes from the Viaduct towards the city and are well worth the walk.

However, my personal favourite is Tanuki's Cave, a Japanese tapas bar located on Queen Street. It has an ambience that makes you feel like you're in Shinjuku, Tokyo, and serves the best yakitori and coldest Orion beer in New Zealand.

Parnell is another area worth visiting for foodies, especially for Non Solo Pizza. This restaurant has a charming little courtyard where you can enjoy good wine, puffy pizza and a truly Italian experience.

Kids

Visit Kelly Tarlton's to learn about penguins and enjoy all the fun underwater exhibits.

For a little bit of excitement and adventure, Rainbow's End amusement park is the perfect place for the whole family to let loose and have some fun.

Stardome Observatory and Planetarium, located in the One Tree Hill Domain, is a great rainy day excursion, with interactive displays to explore beyond the clouds and into space.

Camp

Auckland is a big city, which can make camping a little challenging. Most campsites are on the outskirts of the city.

Takapuna Beach Holiday Park (north Auckland): One of the best places to stay in Auckland, whether you're heading towards the north or south. This campsite offers breathtaking views of the city and Rangitoto Island — its location is unbeatable. Your kids can have a great time playing in the rock pools for hours, making friends with locals who stroll by and watching the yachts and other boats in the channel.

Ōmana Regional Park Cliff Top campground (east Auckland): The grounds are well maintained, and the sunsets are simply breathtaking. Book online through Auckland Council.

Piha Domain Motor Camp (west Auckland): A fantastic choice if you're looking to hit the waves. This west coast beach is known for its black sand. Pull up here for a week and get the kids some surf lessons.

Ambury Regional Park campground (south Auckland): A basic site with wide-open spaces and a farm-like atmosphere. Book online through Auckland Council.

Shop

If you're looking to set up your camper or caravan, Auckland has plenty of options to choose from, from Kathmandu, Torpedo 7, Bunnings and Burnsco to stores like The Warehouse. All these are located at Sylvia Park shopping centre in Mount Wellington — a great choice for those with large campers and caravans, as there are parking spaces that are both wide and long enough to accommodate you.

Dress Smart in Onehunga is an outlet mall and a good place for clothing bargains, especially out-of-season products.

I am personally always keen on a vintage or second-hand store. Back in the sixties, camping gear was special, and it's fun to find those treasures in antiques stores.

Waitākere Ranges

Escape the hustle and bustle of Auckland city and discover the renowned black-sand beach at Piha. There are plenty of exciting outdoor activities to enjoy here, such as walks to waterfalls, horseback riding on the beach, or simply soaking up the sunset.

From the Arataki Visitor Centre, where a magnificent carved pou depicts the ancestors of iwi Te Kawerau ā Maki, you can experience breathtaking views of the Waitākere Ranges Regional Park. The park, covering over 20,000 hectares of land once known as 'The Great Forest of Tiriwa', offers numerous outdoor hikes through beautiful forests to waterfalls and beaches. It is home to a variety of native plants that thrive under the giant kauri trees.

At the northern end of the ranges, Te Henga, also known as Bethells Beach, is a stunning expanse of dark sand, where the Waitākere River meets the wild surf of the Tasman Sea. There's a great walkway along the river, too.

Eat
To the joy of our hungry tummies, we found the Piha Surf Life Saving Club restaurant has a great menu. I can highly recommend their smokehouse board at sunset with a cold bevvie.

Hidden gem
The wild and untamed coast of the west attracts many holidaymakers, but there is one hidden gem that often goes unnoticed: stunning Muriwai Beach.

Like Piha, the beach has black sand that glistens in the sunlight, making for an impressive sight. Surfers and paragliders alike enjoy the strong southwesterly winds that buffet the coastline.

If you or your kids want to learn how to surf, Muriwai Surf School offers surfing lessons and equipment rental. For those interested in nature or photography, the Muriwai gannet colony is a must-see. Every year, between September and April, an impressive number of gannets return to the area from Australia to nest on the cliffs above the sea, making for a stunning photographic opportunity.

Matakana Coast

You can enjoy a variety of outdoor activities in this area north of Auckland, such as fishing in Kawau Bay, surfing at Ōmaha or Tāwharanui, and snorkelling in the famous Goat Island Marine Reserve. Matakana village and Warkworth have everything you need in terms of supermarkets and dining options, and Leigh is a lovely place to check out, too. On the way there or back, enjoy the historical settlement of Pūhoi, with its bohemian vibes and classic pub.

Explore

This area is famous for its farmers' markets. Savour the flavours of the renowned Matakana Village Farmers' Market, or explore the monthly markets at Pūhoi and Wellsford. Matakana celebrates farm-to-fork, and you can speak directly with farmers, growers and producers to learn more about locally made products.

Take the coastal trek at Tī Point, which takes around 2 hours return, with lovely views of Ōmaha, Tāwharanui and Te Hauturu-o-Toi/Little Barrier Island. Discover very cute little blue penguins (kororā) that nest along the shoreline.

Leigh is a charming coastal village that attracts holidaymakers and travellers who come to enjoy the fishing. The wharf is a popular spot for recreational fishers and families.

Experience

Goat Island Marine Reserve is a famous and fully protected marine reserve — the oldest marine reserve in the country and the first in the southern hemisphere. It covers 5 km of coastline with fabulous snorkelling and diving opportunities in safe and shallow conditions. Snorkelling equipment is available for hire, and entrance is free.

Hidden gem

Tāwharanui Regional Park boasts white-sand beaches and lush native forests. The park has several walking trails that cater to different ages and abilities, including the Mangatāwhiri Walk which starts at the Anchor Bay carpark and is a 20-minute meander through regenerating wetlands, offering a chance to catch glimpses of wildlife.

Kids

Snells Beach, Scotts Landing and Whangateau are ideal spots for kids to play in the water and discover new things.

Matakana Country Park is home to Action Ninja World, with its warrior course, flying trapeze, climbing wall and more.

Eat

Whenever we come across oysters, we can't resist them, and enjoy eating them in various ways. Matakana oysters are a pure treat and definitely worth trying.

If you are looking for a place to relax and unwind, I highly recommend the Sawmill Brewery. Take the afternoon off and enjoy their cosy smoko room. This brewery is even more special because it is B Corp certified, which means it is committed to creating a better and more sustainable future — something we encourage and appreciate. And, of course, their hazy beer is delicious.

Camp

Pākiri Beach Holiday Park: Enjoy pristine white sand, the safe and calm Pākiri estuary, and camping sites that are widely spread out, for a peaceful experience.

Whangateau Holiday Park: Right on the waterfront of Whangateau Harbour, between Matakana and Goat Island.

Waiheke Island

The Hauraki Gulf is a popular playground for Auckland weekenders and holidaymakers from further afield. Our family fell in love with the sandy beaches and island vibes of its biggest island, Waiheke. As well as its many wineries, the island is renowned for its local produce, grown by innovative and dedicated farmers who work hard to sustain themselves, many organically. Try the local honey, dairy products, vegetables and, of course, wine.

Getting to Waiheke Island is easy: SeaLink ferries leave from Wynyard Quarter in downtown Auckland, and it's super easy to bring your caravan along for the ride. Just a short 45-minute sail from Auckland, you're on the island.

For us, this is where our New Zealand adventure began! We spent our summer mornings fishing at Man O' War Bay, and our afternoons with a good book on a rug watching the tide drift in and out at our campground. There were also plenty of walks and places for the kids to adventure by bike around the neighbouring bays.

Explore
Get the blood pumping and enjoy the walking trails, ranging from coastal treks to bush walks. A favourite was the Orapiu to Pearl Bay trek, with stunning views of Ponui Island and the Coromandel during your walk along the beautiful coastline on the southern coast of the island.

Waiheke Island has soft, sandy beaches stretching for miles, and all of them are wonderful. Some are busier than others, but if you can't find a park at one, chances are the surrounding spots are just as good. Little Oneroa, Onetangi and Man O' War Bay were our favourites.

Experience
Wild on Waiheke in Onetangi offers a variety of outdoor activities, such as lawn games and archery.

Waiheke Island is famous for its wineries. During our ten-day trip, we visited quite a few! Man O' War, sitting on the water's edge, is the ultimate afternoon excursion. Grab a takeaway bottle to pair with your picnic or sit under the shady trees and enjoy while the kids play in the playground. Our wine pick is the Estate Island Blend. Mudbrick is also a hot favourite, with lots of people visiting the island just to spend the day here. From the restaurant, you can enjoy spectacular views while savouring delicious cuisine. It's a beautiful sunset location, and one we enjoyed as a treat for my husband's birthday.

If you like gin, the Waiheke Distilling Co is a glorious place to enjoy a platter and bespoke cocktail in the sun overlooking Cowes Bay.

Eat
When it comes to food and drink, Waiheke Island has plenty of options to choose from. For the best coffee, head

to the Onetangi Beach Store, where you can enjoy devilishly good sandwiches and Allpress coffee. Don't forget your keep cup for a 50 cent discount.

The island has a supermarket and several excellent food stores to pick up your groceries, so there's no need to over-stock before heading over.

Hidden gem
Dragonfired: Wood-fired pizza on Little Oneroa Beach. Pick up a bottle of your favourite wine from the cellar door and unwind at the beach while the kids hit the playground. Lay a picnic rug and enjoy the view while your pizza cooks in the truck behind.

Kids
The 'Heke restaurant in Onetangi is a fantastic destination for families with young children. Explore and enjoy the amazing distillery and craft brewery while your kids have fun bouncing on the giant pillow or playing in the mud area.

Camp
Poukaraka Flats campground, Whakanewha Regional Park: A family-friendly campground bookable online through Auckland Council. We found a little nook with a picnic table surrounded by native trees, just a short walk to the clean, flush-toilet facilities and fresh drinking water.

Raw fish

My grandfather would often bring home fresh fish and make this dish during my childhood. I have also experimented with the base recipe and given it my own special twist. It's best made with fresh snapper or tarahiki and has a punchy, zesty, creamy flavour that is sure to please.

500 g (1 lb 2 oz) fresh white fish, such as snapper or tarakihi
juice of 1 lemon
2 limes
1 green habanero chilli
½ red capsicum
½ red onion
2:1 mixture of water and white vinegar, for pickling the onion
1 teaspoon brown sugar
400 ml (14 fl oz) can coconut cream
salt and pepper, to taste
corn chips, to serve
bunch of coriander, to garnish

Tips
- Remember to keep the dish refrigerated until serving.
- If you don't want this to be spicy, omit the habanero.

Cut the fish into 2.5 cm x 1 cm slivers and layer them in a serving bowl. Squeeze the lemon juice and the juice of one of the limes over the fish, then refrigerate.

Blister the habanero chilli and capsicum over a flame or hot barbecue until blackened. Let them cool in a covered bowl. When cool, remove the skin and seeds if desired, and dice.

Thinly cut the red onion into moons and place into a bowl with the vinegar/water mixture and brown sugar to pickle for 20 minutes.

Add the can of coconut cream to the fish, along with the diced habanero chilli and capsicum.

Peel the other lime and divide into segments, exposing the flesh. Make incisions in each segment along either side of the membrane to release the flavour. Place onto the fish with a seasoning squeeze of lime, and salt and pepper to taste.

The dish is now ready to serve, but it's even better to let it rest in the fridge for 20–30 minutes. The longer it sits, the softer the fish becomes. You can serve it on corn chips or on its own, topped with pickled onions and garnished with coriander.

Waikato

The Waikato region offers a plethora of nature activities to enjoy. The region is known for its rich agriculture, the famous Waikato River and the stunning Hamilton Gardens, which boast an impressive collection of themed gardens. There are also lots of smaller, boutique gardens around the region, from lavender fields to sculpture gardens and areas of native bush.

Coromandel Peninsula

The Coromandel Peninsula is a beautiful destination for nature enthusiasts and a popular holiday spot for many North Islanders. If you enjoy spending time in the great outdoors and love the beach, then this is the perfect place for you to explore. The long, indented coastline of the peninsula offers excellent fishing spots that are definitely worth checking out, and there are many beautiful beaches on the east coast.

During the summer months, you can visit farmers' markets, go kayaking and spend lazy days at the beach. My family and I were thrilled to explore the area after enduring months of drizzly, cold weather. We were excited to get our inflatable boat on the water, and ended up having lots of fun using it around the peninsula.

Tip
Allow plenty of time for traffic as roads and towns around the peninsula get very busy, especially during peak months.

Thames

The township of Thames, originally known as Grahamstown, is a colonial settlement at the base of the Coromandel Range. The Kauaeranga Valley is a particular highlight, with its magnificent scenery and opportunities for hiking and camping.

Explore
Billygoat Falls (Atuatumoe Falls) is the tallest waterfall in the North Island at 180 metres high, although only parts of it can be seen. To reach it, take the first track on your right at the Kauaeranga Valley road-end carpark. On the short walk to Billygoat Landing, you will enjoy good views of the waterfall.

The Billygoat Circuit is a popular 4–5 hour walk that offers a dramatic glimpse of the falls. Another popular walk is to the summit of The Pinnacles, 759 metres high and offering breathtaking, panoramic views of the southern Coromandel's bush-clad mountains and coastline.

Paeroa, south of Thames, is famous for its soft drink, Lemon & Paeroa. Apart from being the home of L&P, the town also boasts a rich history. Make sure to stop off and take a fun picture with the giant bottle before exploring the various vintage stores.

Experience
If you're a history buff and an aviation enthusiast, you'll find The Aviator Experience in Thames very exciting. As a pilot, Lockie was eager to explore the different simulators that can fly up to 16 different aircraft, including helicopters.

Eat
I absolutely love cheese platters and the kids have a strong love for all sorts

of cheese, too, so The Cheese Barn at Matatoki was the perfect stop for us. On the Hauraki Rail Trail, 10 km from Thames, it's a convenient place to call into for lunch and a stretch.

Camp
Dickson Holiday Park: Located close to the seashore and surrounded by lush bush and birdsong with a stream running by it.

Kauaeranga Valley DOC campsites: Handy to nearby walks, beaches and fishing spots.

Coromandel township

The northern Coromandel is a treasure trove of remote natural beauty that offers a plethora of activities for visitors. The charming Coromandel township, nestled on a peaceful harbour, is a hub for talented artists, foodies and nature enthusiasts. The uncrowded coastline nearby provides access to a variety of walking tracks, as well as fishing, kayaking, swimming, snorkelling and horse riding. With a great variety of DOC camping sites available, this slice of paradise is an ideal location for camping.

Explore
Over the other side of the peninsula from Coromandel town is New Chums Beach, considered one of the top beaches in New Zealand. It's definitely worth dedicating a day to explore the surrounding beaches of Whangapoua and Matarangi, too.

Experience
Fishing can be a very rewarding experience all around the peninsula. I recommend checking out Mussel Barge Snapper Safaris, based at Te Kouma, just south of Coromandel township, for day tours and local fishing expertise.

Kids
Jump on the Driving Creek Railway, where you'll traverse a regenerating native forest up to the so-called EyeFull Tower. The tour combines nature, history and engineering in a trip which takes just over an hour, making it perfect for families. Your rail guide will share the inspiring story of potter Barry Brickell, who replanted over 27,000 native trees on the land, to restore it to its pre-European state. Driving Creek also has other fun experiences to enjoy, including a zipline through the forest and pottery displays.

The Waterworks, on the 309 Road inland from Coromandel, is an impressive interactive outdoor park that offers children a fun and creative play-world. It features numerous swings and a giant clock made from various bits and pieces that showcases remarkable engineering and ingenuity. What makes this park so cool is that everything here has been repurposed into something new for the kids to enjoy.

Eat
Make your way to Kūaotunu and try the poke bowl at Luke's Kitchen.

Camp

Colville Bay Motel and Campground: A popular camping location near the historic settlement of Colville, north of Coromandel township.

Shelly Beach TOP 10 Holiday Park: Get ready to fire up the barbecue and relax in this beautiful camping spot at Shelly Beach. Picturesque grassy grounds and stunning views of the Hauraki Gulf.

Kūaotunu Campground: Over the hill from Coromandel, on the east coast of the peninsula, this lovely campground is a stone's throw from the beach where you can enjoy diving, surfcasting and boating. Kayaks are available for hire. Camping is lush in the 1.8 hectares of park-like surroundings.

Waikawau Bay DOC campsite: This camp is located just a short walk from the beach, and is spacious and family-friendly. The unspoiled Waikawau Bay is an excellent spot to unwind on the beach and indulge in fishing, swimming, kayaking or exploring.

Stony Bay DOC campsite: A spacious campsite by the coast with lush grass and great facilities. From here you can walk or mountain-bike along the Coromandel Coastal Walkway to Fletcher Bay. It's also a popular spot for diving.

Fantail Bay DOC campsite: Enjoy a serene camping experience surrounded by beautiful native trees. Toilets and cold showers only.

Port Jackson DOC campsite: At the northern tip of the peninsula, this campsite is situated right at the water's edge, on a beautiful beach. The Muriwai Coastal Walk takes you up the headland towards Wharekaiatua Pā and offers breathtaking views of the coast.

Fletcher Bay DOC campsite: An oceanfront campsite hidden amongst trees. This area is great for water activities.

Hahei

One of my favourite places is Hahei — I love its relaxed atmosphere, gorgeous beaches and welcoming people. Hahei is a fantastic base from which to explore Cathedral Cove, and is just 9 km away from the mind-blowing Hot Water Beach.

Explore

We blew up our True Kit inflatable the moment we pulled into camp, with intentions of catching snapper for dinner from our little boat and exploring the beautiful little hidden gems of this area. The Te Whanganui-A-Hei (Cathedral Cove) Marine Reserve is located nearby, and currently the only way to visit this beautiful cove is from the water: by kayak, boat tour or private boat. I highly recommend taking an excursion to enjoy the natural beauty of this cove that has been admired by visitors for centuries.

Our little boat was also perfect for exploring the beautiful and clear waters surrounding Whale Cave.

If you have a stand-up paddleboard, paddle out and watch the sunrise — a truly extraordinary way to start the day.

Take a leisurely stroll from Hahei Beach to Te Pare Point Historic Reserve. You'll be surrounded by stunning natural scenery and be able to explore the remnants of two ancient Maori pā.

Be astonished by Hot Water Beach. This unique destination is renowned for the thermal water which bubbles up from beneath the sand. Don't forget to take a spade; you can hire them from the general store or the caravan park. It's a bit of a workout to dig your natural spa, but you can enjoy it for two hours on either side of low tide. This beach is also an excellent spot for surfing.

Eat
We were fortunate enough to catch some snapper which we used to make zesty tacos (recipe on page 104).

If you feel like a beer, The Pour House is the place to go for a refreshing summer drink and some snacks. They also serve delicious gin with an amazing platter.

Little Blue Kitchen offers a fresh take on breakfast and brunch, along with great coffee and delicious filled bagels.

Hahei Eatery & Ice Cream is renowned for its great fish and chips and long-neck milkshakes. My husband recommends the works burger for those who love a bit of everything.

For something fancy or a special occasion, The Church Bistro offers divine food.

If you want a good breakfast at Hot Water Beach, head to the Hot Waves cafe. Their beet benny (eggs Benedict with beetroot hollandaise) is incredibly delicious.

Camp
Hahei Beach Resort: Wake up to the beautiful beach right at your doorstep. The extensive resort offers numerous nooks and crannies to relax in, and almost every path leads straight to the beach. We could easily wheel our little boat down to launch it at first light. Riley and Alba loved heading out with Dad each day. After a day out on the blue, you can come back and soak in the hot tub that overlooks the beach. During summers, you can indulge in delicious burgers from the onsite food trucks, and wake up to an Allpress coffee from the onsite cafe.

Tip
Splash out and book a prime beachfront site — you won't regret it.

Hot Water Beach TOP 10 Holiday Park: Another great option, located just inland from the beach and with great facilities, including a new pool.

Fish tacos

The perfect afternoon meal for our family is a round of fish tacos made with freshly caught snapper or tarakihi. This dish is easy to prepare and has a lot of flavour from simple ingredients.

For the pickled cabbage:
1½ cups water
1½ cups apple cider vinegar
1 teaspoon salt
2 teaspoons sugar
pinch red pepper flakes (optional)
2 cloves garlic, sliced
2 teaspoons Sichuan peppercorns
½ red cabbage, finely sliced

For the fish:
1 long red chilli
125 g (4½ oz) tempura flour
180 ml (6 fl oz) ice-cold water
pinch of salt and pepper
500 ml (17 fl oz) rice bran oil (or other high-smoke-point oil)
350 g (12 oz) (4 fillets) snapper, cut into bite-sized pieces
½ cup plain flour, for dusting

To serve:
6 flour tortillas
bunch of coriander
3 tablespoons lime juice

To make the pickled cabbage, place all the ingredients apart from the cabbage into a saucepan and bring to a simmer for 3–4 minutes. Remove from the heat and pour over the cut cabbage.

To prepare the fish, char the chilli over a flame until it's blackened. Cover it in a bowl, and let it sweat for 5 minutes.

Uncover the chilli and rub the blackened skin with your fingers to remove it. Don't worry if some blackened bits remain — they add a nice flavour. Roughly chop the chilli and set it aside.

Mix the tempura flour, cold water and seasoning in a bowl to make a batter.

Heat oil in a wok or pot for deep-frying. Test the temperature with a small drop of batter. If bubbles dance around the batter, it's ready for the fish.

Dust the fish pieces in flour, then dunk them into the batter. Fry the fish in small batches, avoiding overcrowding. Place each batch on scrunched paper towels to drain excess oil.

To serve, heat the tortillas over a flame. Charring adds a nice smoky touch. Assemble each taco with some pickled cabbage and fish, and top with chilli, coriander and lime juice.

Tairua

Tairua is a delightful little town, situated on a beautiful harbour and offering a wonderful setting for beach activities. It is a favourite spot for surfing and swimming. Locals and returning holidaymakers recommend walking to the peak of Mount Paku — the summit provides a 360-degree view from the Aldermen Islands around to The Pinnacles. The village lies along the estuary, and the main ocean beach is a short walk around the harbour's edge.

Explore
Pauanui is over the water from Tairua, and is renowned for having one of the longest beaches in the region. The Pauanui Trail is a 10 km loop around the estuary with scenic rest stops, and the Pauanui Waterfall track offers a delightful 20-minute bush walk suitable for kids.

Experience
Tours run from Tairua to the Aldermen Islands (Ruamaahu), a chain of islands located around 20 km off the coast of Tairua. This is home to native species including tuatara, and the surrounding waters are a top diving destination.

Slipper Island (Whakahau) is just a 15-minute boat ride from Tairua. Take a picnic and head there for the day, enjoying the public reserve at the southern end of Home Bay, or stay at Slipper Island Resort. The island has a fascinating Māori and European history.

Camp
Tairua Campground: This picturesque campground provides a family-oriented camping experience. A short walkway leads to the harbour.

Whangamatā

Whangamatā is home to one of New Zealand's most famous surf breaks and has been voted as the best beach in New Zealand. Surf enthusiasts can indulge in the left-hand breaks of their dreams but if you're keen to just chill out there are plenty of lovely cafes to enjoy.

Explore
Hit the beach: sometimes a good book, sandcastles and watermelon are all you need to make for a good day or two.

Spend the day at the Wentworth Valley, a beautiful recreational area featuring walks and campsites.

Experience
Take in the tranquillity of calm waters and pristine white sand of the large estuary from a stand-up paddleboard. Glide along, enjoying the watery scene and spot stingrays that often sunbathe in the shallow waters. Book through Surfsup if you don't have your own board.

Camp
Opoutere Coastal Camping: It is so nice to enjoy and support a small, private campground like this one. This is back-to-basics camping in the forest. Free cold showers; hot showers are available for $1.

Waikato

Explore

Te Awa River Ride is a scenic 65 km cycling and walking path following the Waikato River from Ngāruawāhia to Lake Karapiro, showcasing the stunning natural beauty of the region. The path features lakes, rivers, waterfalls, bridges and elevated boardwalks, offering a world-class experience for the whole family.

Experience the beauty of the Blue Spring by taking a walk along the Te Waihou Walkway near Putāruru, a 4.7 km trail alongside a stream which is so clear and blue it looks almost electric. The Blue Spring is the source of 60 per cent of New Zealand's bottled water and gets its stunning blue colour from being filtered through fine sand for over a century.

Experience

At the Waitomo Glowworm Caves, take a boat ride through the glowworm grotto and explore the cave on foot. There are also several other caves to visit.

Zealong Tea Estate is the only place in New Zealand that grows organic, award-winning tea. You can tour the vast tea fields, indulge in a tea ceremony, or have a light lunch or high tea. You can even take some tea with you on your travels to enjoy under the stars.

Eat

Looking for a chill spot to kick back and enjoy a tasty toastie and some killer coffee? Look no further than The Lost Boys! This Hamilton cafe and bar has a totally retro vibe that you're gonna love. And don't even get me started on their sausage rolls — they're darn good! The relish they serve on the side is so tasty, I was practically begging for the recipe.

Smash burgers are taking over the burger scene, and for good reason — they are worthy of the hype. The Last Place Bar is where it's at when it comes to the perfect sloppy, oozy and satisfying smash burger. It's a great spot for the whole fam to chow down and have a good time.

When it's pizza night, I always go for Sal's New York-style pizza; it's a franchise, so once you fall in love you will spot it throughout the country. My personal favourites are mushrooms and pepperoni. Grab a box and enjoy it down by the river.

Mexico is a Mexican-themed restaurant chain with an urban twist. Margaritas, tacos and a great kids' menu too. Don't miss the fried chicken.

Manuka Brothers' Coffee is an inventive coffee shop and roastery. They use mānuka wood to roast their beans, which gives their coffee a distinct and exceptional taste. It is a must-try for any coffee lover.

Kids

We had a great day at Hamilton Zoo, which has a lovely landscaped park and lots of interesting animal friends to meet.

Camp

Lake Hakanoa Motor Caravan Park, Huntly: Lovely, well-maintained grounds and friendly hosts welcome you to this lakefront campground.

Freedom camp

Waikato council allows freedom camping is most areas. You can park your self-contained vehicle overnight on a public road, as long as there are no other restrictions, like time limits.

Carpark of Porritt Stadium, Hamilton: Offers freedom camping for certified self-contained vehicles.

Tui Park, Piopio: No time restrictions. Self-contained, non-self-contained.

Benneydale Domain: Southeast of Te Kūiti, deep in the countryside. Self-contained vehicles only.

Te Waitere Reserve: Both self-contained and non-self-contained vehicles can overnight here, on the Kawhia Harbour.

Te Anga Road Scenic Lookout: On the road out to the coast from Waitomo, three spots for self-contained vehicles.

The Grape Escape, Tamahere: Enjoy the wide-open spaces, birds singing and lush greenery.

Matamata

Matamata is a charming small town which is also an important centre of the horse-racing industry. It's renowned for its horse studs, and many famous racehorses have been bred here.

Matamata is also close to some of the most beautiful natural attractions in the region, including the Wairere Falls, the highest waterfall in the North Island. The view from the top of the falls to the valley below is breathtaking.

Experience

Whether or not you're a fan of *The Lord of the Rings*, visiting the Hobbiton movie set near Matamata is an amazing experience. The short bus ride to the farm is an adventure in itself, then you'll be taken on a walking tour around the movie set and see the intricate detailing up close. For an immersive hobbit experience, you can stay in a hobbit hole.

Camp

Brock's Place: Only 1.5 km from Hobbiton is a beautiful countryside stay where you can experience farm life on a budget. You won't find any power facilities around, but don't worry, you can still take a hot shower for just $2. Enjoy the rolling hills and peacefulness of this place.

Da Barn: Quickly gaining popularity thanks to its welcoming owners, fresh countryside air, wide open spaces and powered camping sites, making it a lovely spot to enjoy the evening golden glow.

Cambridge

The area around Cambridge is known for its lush pastures, but there is plenty of outdoor fun such as water sports and bush walks to enjoy, too. It's a perfect base from which to explore the Waikato.

Experience
Get up close with very cute alpacas at Alpaca Experience, about 10 minutes' drive south of Cambridge. The 25-hectare organic farm also offers extensive rural views.

The Boatshed Kayaks will take you on a kayak or paddleboard adventure, or you can hire equipment and take yourself for a paddle. Discover Lake Karapiro's hidden waterfalls and join the glowworm kayak trip for stunning twilight views.

Eat
Podium cafe, with its beautiful location at the Mighty River Domain on Lake Karapiro, offers high-quality food and coffee. Lovely place to stop in.

Camp
Cambridge TOP 10 Holiday Park: The kids can have fun in the play area and jumping pillow, while also enjoying the large, grassy grounds in which to ride their scooters or bikes.

Freedom camp
Keeley Recreational Reserve: Vehicles have to be self-contained but there are toilets on site. A great spot by Lake Karapiro.

Raglan

The west coast township of Raglan is the Waikato's favourite beach town, and I have to say, it's a world of fun! There are so many activities to choose from, from kayaking to fishing and hiking, but what most flock here for is the surfing. Raglan is home to New Zealand's most popular surf break, at the beloved Manu Bay.

Explore
The 55-metre Bridal Veil Falls are located only 10 minutes from Raglan. The walk to the falls is easily doable for kids, and I carried my bub in a front-pack. The climb can be slippery, though.

For adventurers, Mount Karioi offers a great hike — on a clear day, you can spot Taranaki Maunga, one of the highest mountains in the North Island, from the summit. Te Toto Gorge Track is also worth considering if you are interested in history: this route was once frequently used by Māori, and you can still see remnants of stone garden walls in some places.

For a fun day at the beach, head to Ocean Beach where you can swim, body-board or catch a surf lesson at the Raglan Surf School.

One of my favourite things to do when visiting a new town is to see it from its highest point. That's why we took a short drive to the Michael Hope Lookout above

Ngarunui Beach. The loop road offered jaw-dropping views of the waves peeling away below — truly a sight to behold. We took our cheese platter and some wine to enjoy watching the day fade away.

Hidden gem
Raglan Kayak & Paddleboard will take you to explore the region's intriguing Limestone Coast on sit-on-top kayaks. You'll visit secluded bays, black-sand beaches and cultural sites with a colourful history.

Eat
A fun and casual restaurant, George's Beach Club offers great wood-fired pizza and an ambience perfect for a post-surf dinner. Kids can even enjoy their meals while fooling around on table swings.

Whatawhata Berry Farm, on the road between Hamilton and Raglan, is known for its mouthwatering real-fruit ice cream. My children enjoyed checking out the farm animals and playing on the playground, but it was the pick-your-own-strawberries experience that they really thrived on — learning about garden-to-plate. Now we have a strawberry and a parsley plant growing in our Kombi!

Camp
Raglan Holiday Park: Sitting in a prime location on a peninsula in Raglan Harbour, it's almost entirely surrounded by water. The beach is just a two-minute walk away, and guests can enjoy amenities such as a barbecue area and children's playground.

Taupō

I love Taupō! Located in the heart of the North Island, this beautiful town offers a wide range of natural attractions that are sure to leave you in awe.

Taupō is the largest lake in New Zealand, and you can explore its many bays and coves by taking a boat tour or going kayaking. You can also try your luck at golfing literally into the lake.

For thrill-seekers, Taupō offers raging rapids that are perfect for white-water rafting. The Tongariro River is a popular spot for rafting, and many tour operators offer guided trips. If you're looking for a more relaxing experience, Taupō has plenty of thermal hot springs where you can soak in the warm waters and enjoy the natural surroundings.

At the southern end of the lake lies the Tongariro National Park, a UNESCO World Heritage Site (see page 164), where a range of short and long tramps reveal the stunning volcanic landscapes and unique flora and fauna.

Explore

At the point where Otumuheke Stream's warm geothermal waters flow into the Waikato River, natural springs create a hot spot for bathers. Immerse yourself under a waterfall or in the natural rock pools while enjoying the views of the deep green, crystal-clear waters of the mighty Waikato. The bathing area is located in the Spa Thermal Park, next to the starting point of the Huka Trail, which leads to Huka Falls.

The breathtaking natural wonder of Huka Falls makes it one of New Zealand's most popular attractions. Take a leisurely stroll along the Waikato River to one of the many lookout points that offer stunning views. Begin at the Huka Falls carpark and cross the bridge over the falls, then turn left and follow the well-graded track — ideal for families with children.

For a family-friendly walk, the Rimu Walk in Pureora Forest Park northwest of Taupō is an excellent option. The loop walk takes you through dense rimu forest, with plenty of opportunities to spot a variety of birdlife along the way. The track leads to a viewpoint that offers breathtaking views of the forest and Mount Pureora.

Taupō is a great destination for fishers. The region is famous for trout fishing since the introduction of brown and rainbow trout in the late 1800s. Tūrangi is the gold standard for trout fishing in New Zealand and worldwide. The clean, clear waters of Lake Taupō offer an abundance of food sources for trout and there are a number of tributaries to fish in.

For huge, panoramic views of the whole amazing landscape, hike to the top of Mount Tauhara, behind Taupō township.

Experience

The giant Ngātoroirangi Mine Bay rock carvings can only be viewed from the lake. Matahi Brightwell's carvings are considered one of the most extraordinary contemporary

Māori artworks in the country. Choose from several operators to take a cruise along Western Bay to the carvings — a beautiful way to spend your day.

Wairakei Terraces is a relatively new development with adults-only outdoor pools, a terrace walk and spa treatments.

Kids

The AC Baths is a fantastic family-friendly pool that offers a variety of activities. The outdoor leisure pool is particularly impressive, featuring two separate areas designed for toddlers, as well as two hydroslides and a Tarzan swing. The pools are heated using natural hot water and are partly undercover, so you can enjoy a soothing and relaxing day out no matter the weather.

Just across from the lake and shopping strip, the Tongariro South Domain is a lovely green space. The gardens feature a children's railway, as well as a popular playground and a Superloo. (If you're wondering what a Superloo is, it's a community bathroom facility that includes a baby room, with a microwave and hot water for warming up baby bottles. You can also have a hot shower here for a small fee, and towels are included.) There's also a great information centre.

Camp

Lake Taupo Holiday Resort: Offers both powered and non-powered campsites, as well as a luxurious swim-up bar.

Taupo DeBretts Spa Resort: Beautiful private sites and modern new bathrooms. Campers also get discounted access to the adjacent waterpark, which features hydroslides, a kids' water park and a range of hot pools.

Motuoapa Bay Holiday Park: A hidden gem located on the southern shores of Lake Taupō. Licorice Cafe is just a short walk away, and Tūrangi has a supermarket for supplies. The area is great for fishing, and handy to the mountains for skiing or hiking. If you're in the mood for a relaxing soak, Tokaanu Thermal Hot Pools are the nearest.

Motutere Bay TOP 10 Holiday Park: This beautiful peaceful lakeside park is located around 30 km south of Taupō township. It's situated right on the shores of the lake, making it the only place where you can park your vehicle close to the water's edge, so grab some camp chairs, pour yourself a glass of wine and enjoy watching the lake turn to silk at dusk.

Freedom camp

Hipapatua Recreational Reserve: A spacious site, perfect for those who are not self-contained. Fall asleep to the sound of the nearby river.

Mangakino Lakefront Reserve: Lovely lakeside spot on a hydro lake north of Taupō. Plenty of shade and good facilities. It's within walking distance to local shops, and there are excellent walking and biking trails for kids.

Lake Whakamaru Reserve: A picturesque camping spot with lake views, clean toilets, showers and excellent barbecue facilities.

Bay of Plenty/Te Moana-a-Toi

Bay of Plenty, my home region, is a paradise on the east coast of the North Island. It's a place where sandy beaches, friendly locals and a laid-back atmosphere blend to create a memorable camping holiday.

You can explore the bay by boat or take in the coastal drives. Whakatāne is the sunniest town in the region, and Tauranga, the fifth-largest city in New Zealand, boasts a beautiful waterfront location with a rich maritime history.

A stroll along the Strand is a treat for the senses, with stunning waterside scenery, and cute cafes. Nearby is Mount Maunganui, one of the area's most popular beach destinations. The region is also home to Rotorua, which is rich in Māori culture and geysers. Whether you're looking for a relaxing camping holiday or an action-packed adventure, Bay of Plenty has something for everyone.

Waihī and Katikati

During my years living in Auckland, I would frequently drive down to see my friends and family in the Bay of Plenty but I never realised what was right under my nose along the way. Waihī and Katikati are two great small towns that offer plenty of opportunities for exploration. Waihī is known for its sunny weather and goldmining heritage, while Katikati is famous for being the avocado capital of New Zealand.

Explore

The Western Bay Museum in Katikati is home to a variety of fascinating artefacts and has a fun retro atmosphere. Make sure you stop along the road to pick up freshly picked fruit and vegetables, and head to the Katikati Bird Gardens for a picnic lunch.

The Goldfields Railway is one of the must-visit attractions in the area. This vintage train runs between Waihī and Waikino, and is a great way to learn about the rich history of goldmining here. Many relics from the gold-rush days are also on display.

Waihī provides easy access to the Hauraki Rail Trail, via the breathtaking Karangahake Gorge. There's a short loop section which includes two bridges and a 1100-metre railway tunnel that is perfect for the kids.

Experience

Discover Waihī's search for gold at the Gold Discovery Centre. Learn about early miners and their quest for gold and silver at the Waihī Gold Experience, before viewing the modern goldmine site.

Eat

I enjoyed a beautiful platter from The Platter Board in Waihī.

Athenree is a peaceful settlement nestled just across the estuary from Bowentown. The historic homestead there has a lovely cafe in an old station building.

Camp

Sapphire Springs Holiday Park: A wonderful place to camp near Katikati, with an abundance of fun for children, and hot mineral pools.

Bowentown Beach Holiday Park: If you're looking for a quintessential laid-back beach experience, look no further than this campsite at the southern end of the beach. You'll have access to great walks and fishing opportunities, as well as the chance to explore Cave Bay and Anzac Bay. You can also stay in quirky, cute replica Kombi cabins. A major highlight of this campsite is the Allpress coffee available at the onsite coffee shop, where you can also purchase freshly baked sourdough.

Tasman Holiday Park Beachaven: Beachside getaway close to the Waihī Beach township, which has a great pool and a lovely playground. Enjoy breakfast or brunch with an ocean view at nearby cafe Flatwhite.

Dickey Flat DOC campsite: An awesome campsite located next to the Waitawheta River, which is famous for its trout and cool swimming spots.

Freedom camp
Bowentown Domain carpark: A free camp space with payable showers and laundry facilities.

Pōhutukawa Park, Waihī Beach: Listen to the ocean right from your kitchen. (No camping Labour Weekend–Easter.)

Waihī Gorge and Waihī Falls campsites: Lovely riverside camps, but you must be self-contained.

Tauranga and Mount Maunganui

For sandy toes and sunny beaches, look no further than the coastline around Tauranga and Mount Maunganui. This was a hot favourite for my girlfriends and I as teenagers; once we all had our licences we would hit the road for a girls' road-trip during summer, and today it's become a popular destination for more permanent residents seeking a warm climate and coastal living. You can enjoy surfing, paddleboarding, nature walks and great fishing.

The golden beaches and the sound of the rolling waves of the Pacific Ocean make Mount Maunganui an irresistible destination for families seeking seaside serenity and salty breezes. Mount Maunganui is also the perfect starting point for scenic side-trips to Papamoa, Maketū, Pukehina and Whakatāne.

Explore

Take a beach stroll to Moturiki Island, a great place for kids to explore.

Experience the stunning outdoor scenery of McLaren Falls, where there's a beautiful waterfall track, a lake and botanical gardens. The park is beautiful year-round, but the autumn colours are just gorgeous. With kids, be sure to check out the glowworms and Marshalls Animal Park.

Ōtanewainuku Forest is home to some beautiful native bush, many giant rimu trees and lots of birds. Check out the panoramic views from the summit of Mount Ōtanewainuku, out towards East Cape, Mount Tarawera and Rotorua, and across the Mamaku Plateau to Mount Ruapehu. There are a couple of good walking tracks.

Tip

After visiting Ōtanewainuku Forest, unwind in the relaxing hot pools at Smallgusta in Oropi.

Matakana Island is a beautiful place to explore. Just over 20 km long, it's home to a small population of locals and boasts a blend of pine forests, orchards and farmland. The northern shore attracts surfers who travel over by boat or jetski, but you can also visit it on the *Kewpie* (see below).

The Kaituna Wetland Loop walk is an easy stroll that's perfect for families with young children. Beginning and ending at the picnic area, it meanders through the trees of the reserve and the surrounding lush grass.

Experience

Cruise on the iconic 70-year-old *Kewpie*, Tauranga's original harbour-cruise boat, now lovingly restored. You can cruise around the harbour, stop off at Matakana Island and see the bronze statue of Tangaroa at the entrance by Mount Maunganui, as well as spot some wildlife.

Waimarino Kayak Tours offer a variety of outdoor experiences. The Big Kanu adventure will take you into the stunning Mangapapa Canyon at Lake McLaren to see hundreds of glowworms.

Minden Lookout, inland from Te Puna, is one of the top vantage points in the Bay of Plenty region. The lookout is easy to find (drive up Minden Rd) and offers breathtaking views of the countryside and Tauranga Harbour, with plenty of parking for campers. Make sure to have your camera handy.

Te Puna's most popular attraction is its former quarry, transformed more than 20 years ago into a stunning garden and tracks for hikers and bikes. In the butterfly garden, monarchs and admirals emerge from their chrysalises, and kids can enjoy climbing the impressive stone dragon or riding the wooden train.

Hidden gem
The Puketoki Scenic Reserve, inland from Te Puna, is full of secret walking paths that lead to beautiful waterholes and waterfalls for a refreshing cool-off in the summer months.

Eat
My family can't get enough of New Zealand's famous fresh-fruit ice cream during the summer. Whenever we spot one of these stands, we pull over to indulge in rich ice cream made with fresh berries. One of our favourite places is Somerfields Berryfruit Farm in Oropi, a locally owned and family-operated business that offers some of the finest berries in the Bay. Here, you can pick strawberries, buy delicious raspberries, strawberries and blueberries, and enjoy a real-fruit ice cream. It's the perfect destination for a summer family fun-day.

Camp
Mount Maunganui Beachside Holiday Park: Relax and enjoy the great Kiwi camping experience right on the beach at the base of Mauao (Mount Maunganui). Lots of cafes nearby for those seeking coffee and lunch.

Welcome Bay Hot Pools & Campground: A family-owned and -operated swimming-pool complex and camping ground located on the outskirts of Tauranga. The small campground features a natural thermal swimming pool with free access for campers.

Omokoroa TOP 10 Holiday Park: A relaxing and chilled place to unwind and enjoy a cold beer around the pool. A great space for families, with lovely sunset views.

Freedom camp
Omokoroa Domain: Well-maintained and -equipped freedom campsite.

Papamoa

Once a quiet beachside town beloved for its Kiwi baches, Papamoa has transformed into a suburban extension of Tauranga. It still has a beautiful golden stretch of beach perfect for swimming, fishing and paddleboarding.

Eat
The Island brewery and restaurant is within walking distance of the holiday park and has a great menu and cold beers.

Camp
Tasman Holiday Parks Papamoa Beach: This beachfront holiday park has new facilities and a very cool new pool. As a mother to a one-year-old and two other little people, the 'kids' bathroom was a godsend. Enjoy a barbecue on site as the sky turns pink at sunset.

Freedom camp
Stella Place: A lovely place to wake up right near the sea. Must be self-contained.

Te Puke

If you're a fan of kiwifruit, Te Puke is the place for you! It's also a great place to stock up on supplies and take a leisurely stroll down the main street, which is home to many charming local stores, cafes and a historic pub.

Experience
If you're into golf, Te Puke has an excellent course for a day on the green.

Freedom camp
Paengaroa Domain: A handy stop, with plenty of spots available.

Maketū/Pukehina

East of Tauranga lie the little townships of Maketū and Pukehina, where my grandparents used to stay during the summer months. My memories of this place are filled with clear-sky days spent doing the pipi dance with our toes and filling our harakeke baskets with sweet shellfish.

Pukehina Beach is a great place to surf, kite-surf or fish, with underwater reefs and rocks attracting plenty of fish. The long sandspit separates the ocean from an estuary, offering calmer waters.

Eat
Maketū meat pies have been cherished among Kiwis for nearly four decades. Their flaky crust and savoury filling make them a must-try.

Enjoy some fish and chips from the Pukehina Beach Store & Takeaway.

Camp
To escape and disconnect, stay at the Maketū freedom campsite or at the Bledisloe Holiday Park.

Pukehina is also welcoming to freedom campers that are self-contained.

Rotorua

I am thrilled to share with you my hometown of Rotorua, where I spent my childhood and teenage years. It is a place where everyone can have fun. Lake Rotorua is one of many beautiful lakes in the Bay of Plenty, with camping options available at several of them. Returning to Rotorua to share it with my family, I noticed that many new and beautiful attractions have emerged alongside some longstanding ones.

Rotorua has long been loved and renowned for its geothermal wonders, and because there are very few places like it in the world, spending time here is a must. Besides the geothermal activity, Rotorua has a rich Māori presence, providing an opportunity to embrace Māori culture in its truest form.

For thrill-seekers, Rotorua is New Zealand's original outdoor fun park, with a wide range of outdoor activities on offer. There are plenty of creeks and rivers to swim in, and many are thermally heated. And if you're in the mood for some pampering, you can enjoy spa treatments. Rotorua caters to everyone.

Explore

Walk through The Redwoods at Whakarewarewa, just five minutes from the town centre. This forest is renowned for mountain-biking and walking trails for all ages and fitness levels. Bring a picnic, as there are plenty of spots to enjoy. The Redwoods Treewalk is a must-do, with a network of suspended swing bridges between the giant redwood trees. We returned to do this at night, and seeing the trees lit up with lanterns and colourful lights was incredible.

Lake Rotorua is world-famous for its excellent trout fishing. The lake has five tributaries perfect for fly fishing, particularly during summer, as the cicadas are hatching.

Government Gardens is lovely to see on a clear spring day. The Tudor-style building at its centre has a rich history, having served as a bath house, night club and museum. The gardens have some notable landmarks, such as the Blue Baths and the Gardener's Cottage, the oldest surviving heritage building in Rotorua. You can also witness the natural thermal vents at Sulphur Point.

Experience

While you are in Rotorua, you will no doubt hear the tale of lovers Hinemoa and Tūtānekai. Tūtānekai lived on Mokoia Island in the middle of the lake, from where he called out to his lover. Mokoia is now a wildlife refuge, and you can explore the history and cultural significance of the island. Visit the island aboard the Katoa Jet for an exciting ride.

Rotorua is widely known as a hub for Māori culture. Te Arawa is one of the prominent tribes in Rotorua, and the stories and performances depicting their

history can be experienced through the Te Pā Tū journey at the Tamaki Māori Village. At night, you can explore the trails from the pā, an interactive village that connects you with the past, where you can learn Māori waiata/songs, poi and haka, and complete the experience with a modern twists on a traditional hāngī. I absolutely loved the consommé and the smoked eel. You'll leave with a full stomach and a warm heart.

Whakarewarewa Village is the ancestral home of the Tūhourangi Ngāti Wāhiao, who have welcomed guests into their homes and backyards since the mid-1800s, demonstrating how to use the natural geothermal wonders of the valley for cooking, bathing and heating.

At Whakarewarewa you can also witness the eruption of the largest natural geyser in the southern hemisphere, Pōhutu. At the New Zealand Māori Arts and Crafts Institute at Te Puia, skilled carvers and weavers demonstrate their expertise for visitors.

Rotorua is renowned for its thermal pools, and there are many to choose from to suit all budgets, families and adults.

- Polynesian Spa is great for families, with numerous pools at different temperatures. Book a private room overlooking Lake Rotorua for a quiet evening.
- The Secret Spot is Rotorua's newest hot-tub location, near the mountain-bike hub off State Highway 5 at Whakarewarewa. Soothe your adventurous bones with a soak surrounded by peaceful native forest. If you don't have time for a soak in the tubs, try the 'shinny dips' (foot hot tubs) in the café paired with a meal and a beer.
- Immerse yourself in the otherworldly and fascinating geothermal mud pools at Hell's Gate. Enjoy a detoxifying mud bath followed by a hot-pool soak — the water contains a range of healing minerals that will leave you feeling rejuvenated and refreshed.
- Wai Ariki Hot Springs is a new spa sanctuary for adults. This is a luxury retreat that is wonderful for those looking to completely relax and rejuvenate by soaking up thermal minerals.

Hidden gem
When travelling between Rotorua and Taupō, don't miss out on visiting Kerosene Creek, a beloved local spot. This natural creek features a small pond and waterfall where you can relax in water that can reach up to 40°C. The hot water from a natural spring under the earth bubbles up into the calm waters of the creek, which is set amid lush native bush, making it popular among locals and tourists. Best of all, it's free.

Kids
If you're visiting New Zealand, you cannot miss the experience of watching a shearing show. Just 10 minutes from Rotorua city centre lies the famous Agrodome, where for more than four decades, tourists have been entertained

by the world-renowned show featuring a talented cast of animals. There's also a farmyard nursery and farm tour.

Kids will also love the Skyline Rotorua luge track, which I have visited over many years. The luge is an ingenious combination of a go-cart and toboggan, powered by gravity. There's a range of tracks with thrilling twists and turns, suitable for all ages (smaller kids can ride with adults). You can also luge at night under coloured LED lights. You also get panoramic views from the gondola up the hill; once you reach the top, enjoy a coffee at the cafe while the kids go wild on the luge.

On the Rotorua lakefront is an excellent new playground for kids, with views of Mokoia Island. It is a lovely place for a stroll, cycle or afternoon ice cream from Lady Janes (see next column). I fondly remember coming here for the Saturday markets and a fun time on the old playground. Now the playground has been redeveloped, and the grassy picnic area has also been redeveloped and landscaped — the kids loved the dual flying foxes. The lakefront is within walking distance from the city centre and the restaurants of 'Eat Streat'.

Kuirau Park is also close to the city centre, and is a great place to witness bubbling geothermal activity for free. Stroll around and feel like you are having an outdoor steam facial.

Eat
While in Rotorua, trying food cooked in a hāngī (earth oven) is an absolute must! For a road trip picnic, Capers Café has a great selection of 'ready-to-go' items. You can also grab a coffee and explore their deli shop while you're there.

Lady Janes Ice Cream Parlour is a must-visit spot for me. It's where I had my very first waffle cone with peanuts, cream and chocolate sauce, and it's been serving up sweetness to Rotorua for over 40 years.

We love to try something new, and Saigon '60s is a Vietnamese eatery which has a great range of yummy, fresh salads, soups and noodle and rice dishes.

If you're heading out to the Blue Lake, grab a quick bite to eat at La Bonne Poulette at the Tarawera turnoff. Love their heart rolls.

Camp
Rotorua Thermal Holiday Park: A great place to park up. Free on-site hot pools and swimming pool.

All Seasons Holiday Park, Hannahs Bay: Fun dinosaur playground, spacious sites, great for those seeking lakeside fishing.

Waikite Valley Hot Pools: This has long been a favourite place of mine; unwind in the thermal hot pools with camping on site, overlooking farmland.

Freedom camp
Hamurana Reserve Campground is a quiet lakeside parking area with plenty of room, lovely trees and sufficient toilets.

Lake Rotoiti

The Okere Falls are on the Kaituna River, which runs between Rotorua/Rotoiti and Tauranga, and are popular for rafting and kayaking. There is easy access to various viewpoints along the Okere Falls Track, which leads to impressive rock caves. The grassy area at the start of the track has picnic tables and toilets, and the trout pool at the end of the track is a popular fishing spot. Okere Falls Store serves excellent coffee and offers stunning views.

Explore
Hinehopu/Hongi's Track loops from Lake Rotoiti to Lake Rotoehu through native forest, including a sacred matai tree. Enjoy the beautiful Korokitewao Bay at the Lake Rotoiti end.

Hidden gem
The Lake Rotoiti Hot Pools in Manupirua Bay have been a beloved attraction for Māori and Europeans for hundreds of years. Today, visitors can indulge in the various hot pools, of differing temperatures, while enjoying the view of Lake Rotoiti's clear waters. We took our little inflatable boat, but you can also take a water taxi from the VR Rotorua Lake Resort in Ōkawa Bay.

Camp
Lake Rotoiti Holiday Park: A friendly park located on the lakefront. Clean and tidy facilities include a jetty, boat ramp, kayaks, hall and playground. It's an easy walk to the Okere Falls Store, bush walks and the Kaituna River.

Lake Ōkāreka

Lake Ōkāreka is a popular destination for swimming, waterskiing, yachting, kayaking, waka ama (outrigger canoeing) and trout fishing. Additionally, you can enjoy walks around the lake that offer breathtaking views of the surrounding area. Other beautiful lakes nearby include Tikitapu (Blue Lake), Rotokākahi (Green Lake) and Tarawera.

Experience
The Kayak Glow Worm Tour is a must-do. It runs every evening and includes sunset kayaking along Lake Ōkāreka's shores. Your guide will lead you through small caves that are home to glowworm constellations.

Camp
Lake Ōkāreka DOC campsite: Located on the northern shores of Lake Ōkāreka, just 15 minutes from central Rotorua. You can enjoy fishing and kayaking, there's a great playground at nearby Boyes Beach and a trail to a jumping rock close by. Toilets, cooking shelter and tables provided.

Blue Lake TOP 10 Holiday Park: A real paradise, conveniently located close to the famous Whakarewarewa Redwood Forest and its mountain bike trails and walking paths.

Camp lamb burger

There is something special about New Zealand lamb, and put into a burger or pita pocket it makes a great lakeside meal while camping.

Tzatziki burger sauce
1 cucumber
1 cup natural Greek yoghurt
1 tablespoon chopped mint
2 tablespoons lemon juice
½ tablespoon olive oil
1 garlic clove, grated
pinch of salt

500 g (1 lb 2 oz) lamb mince
½ raw beetroot, grated
½ tablespoon American mustard
½ tablespoon salt
1 tablespoon freshly ground pepper
4 rashers bacon
100 g (3½ oz) feta cheese
4 fresh burger buns
butter, to spread
sliced onions and tomato, burger pickles, rocket, etc, for toppings

To make the sauce, finely grate the cucumber and squeeze out the excess water in a tea towel.

Combine the cucumber, yoghurt, mint, lemon juice, olive oil, garlic and salt in a mixing bowl.

For the burger patties, combine the lamb, beetroot, mustard, salt and pepper in a bowl. Squeeze to combine, then divide the meat into four even balls. Toss each one from hand to hand to bind; the harder the better for a good bind, so you don't need to use egg or breadcrumbs.

Place on a hot barbecue plate and press them flat. Cook for 4–5 minutes before flipping. At the same time, cook the bacon on the hot plate until it's crispy.

Just as the patties are finishing, crumble some feta cheese onto each patty and let it melt. Add the cut buns to the grill and lightly toast, then butter.

Spread the tzatziki on the bottom of each bun using the back of a spoon. Top it with a patty, then add onions, bacon, tomato, burger pickles (a must!) and a handful of rocket. I love a healthy squeeze of tomato sauce on the top bun before closing the lid.

Whakatāne

Whakatāne is a treasure trove of adventure and excitement for the entire family, whether you're exploring the great bushwalks nearby or discovering the rich marine life offshore. Over the hill, sunny Ōhope awaits, with its beautiful beaches and relaxed vibes. Oh, and I was born here!

Explore

Whakatāne is home to so many bike tracks and wonderful scenic walks for all fitness levels it really is hard to pick just a few to share. The Ngā Tapuwae o Toi Trail takes you through three breathtaking scenic reserves: Kohi Point, Ōhope and Mokorua. If you plan to complete the 16 km round trip, it's better to walk clockwise — the track is much more challenging if you go in the opposite direction. Don't forget to bring your camera along to capture the amazing sights and scenes along the way, especially for the lookout over Ōhope Beach.

Hidden gem

Whirinaki Te Pua-a-Tāne Conservation Park is a fascinating destination that combines monstrous trees, rushing rivers and diverse habitats. It is one of the most significant forests in New Zealand, boasting spectacular scenery, and is located within easy driving distance of Whakatāne.

Enjoy a shaded picnic under the towering tōtara trees, or take a short or long walk. The Arohaki Lagoon is worth a visit: it's home to several species of rare birds, including blue duck/whio, North Island kākā, red- and yellow-crowned kākāriki, kiwi and kererū.

Experience

New Zealand is renowned for whitewater rafting, and Riverbug provides a great opportunity for first-timers to give it a go inland from Whakatāne on the Rangitaiki River. It's a fun way to hit the rapids and discover hidden canyons and cascading waterfalls, while enjoying the beautiful river environment. Great for families with children aged five and up.

Kids

Get the kids walking on a self-guided one-hour scavenger hunt in search of the 10 life-size bronze kiwi statues dotted around Whakatāne.

The short track to Wairere Falls winds through rocky terrain and tree roots, making it an ideal adventure for young explorers. Along the path, you'll discover natural pools where you can have a snack while taking in the cascading waterfalls.

Eat

Julians Berry Farm is a must-visit if you're in Whakatāne. Every year, flocks of locals and visitors come here during the summer months to enjoy its fresh-fruit ice cream, plus kids can have a great time picking field-ripened berries and feeding the baby animals. There's also an on-site playground. Don't miss this roadie stop! Open late September to the end of February.

Gibbo's On The Wharf is an excellent fish and chip shop that offers a variety of freshly caught fish and seafood to enjoy right there on the wharf — or take it with you to the beach.

Camp
Awakeri Hot Springs Holiday Park: Southwest of Whakatāne. A hot favourite for many years due to its lush location and naturally heated pools.

Thornton Beach Holiday Park: An excellent camping spot away from the bustle. Great beach access and lovely grassy sites.

Whakatāne Holiday Park: Located in the heart of Whakatāne, this holiday park offers great facilities and convenient access to the town centre, including a scenic bike track along the river.

Pikowai Camping Ground: On the beachfront between Whakatāne and Tauranga. Great for beach fishing and swimming.

Freedom camp
McAlister St carpark: An overnight spot for self-contained campers.

Lake Aniwhenua: About an hour's drive south of Whakatāne, on the road to Murupara. It is a great place for kids, as it has an awesome playground. It's stay-by-donation, and it's definitely worth donating to stay at one of the best freedom camping spots in the area.

Ōhope

I love Ōhope. The sunshine, surf and charming cafes make it an easy and relaxing place to be. I have been driving through Ōhope during my holidays for most of my life; my family would often stop for a coffee and a quick leg-stretch before driving another 2 hours to our family's bach. Ōhope boasts a beautiful beach that's perfect for surfing. It's also a great spot for camping, with stunning views of Whale and White islands (Moutohorā and Whakaari).

Experience
Fishing is hugely popular along this coastline. For a bit of DIY, head to the Port Ōhope wharf to cast your own line.

You could also head out with a charter operator. Pacific Coast Adventures provides half- or full-day inshore fishing trips, along with rock fishing, surfcasting, shellfish gathering and long-lining.

Gambler Fishing Charters specialises in White Island kingfish but can also target other species such as snapper, tarakihi and kahawai.

Ōhiwa Fishing Charters offers trips for fishers of all levels, departing daily from Ōhope Wharf.

Eat
Port Ōhope General Store: Within walking distance of the holiday park, with great coffee and wicked burgers.

Tio Ōhiwa Oyster Farm will not disappoint, if you like these shellfish. I recommend a Kiwi classic: battered oysters in a white-bread sandwich.

Camp
Ōhope TOP 10 holiday park: All you could dream of for a classic beachside stay. Seafront sites, fun waterslide and an outdoor cinema.

Tasman Holiday Parks Ōhiwa Beach: Pull up, light the barbecue and send the kids off to the bouncy pillow. This is a place for utter relaxation, right on the water.

Freedom camp
Ōhiwa Harbour wharf: For self-contained caravans or vans. This spot is popular for surfcasting from the beach or launching your boat from the ramp. Try night fishing for trevally, and some have even had success with kingfish.

Te Kaha

Te Kaha is a tranquil fishing and diving area which offers breathtaking ocean views from wild, stony beaches where giant pōhutukawa trees provide shade. Te Kaha is great for surfcasting, and kids can enjoy kayaking in the safe bays or explore the rock pools, discovering a variety of sea life. A beach bonfire is the perfect way to end the day, while watching the sunset and enjoying your catch.

Explore
Maraetai/Schoolhouse Bay is a great spot for families to swim in calm waters. Inland, the Raukūmara Range offers dense forests and steep valleys for an adventure. Take a leisurely stroll along a bush trail or challenge yourself with a horse trek through the rugged terrain. For thrill-seekers, take a jet-boat ride on the Mōtū River, which offers wild scenery and a spell-binding sense of isolation.

Hidden gem
The Whinray Scenic Reserve Track, inland off the Waioeka Gorge road to Gisborne (State Highway 2), offers a great dose of nature. From the Mōtū Falls carpark, a majestic swing bridge will transport you to a world of natural beauty. The track follows on old coach road.

Eat
Te Kaha Holiday Park has a fish and chip shop and café.

Te Kaha Beach Hotel overlooks the boat ramp, and as well as its own restaurant it runs a small dairy offering takeaway options and groceries.

The Nuthouse Cafe is a wonderful spot to stop by for a cup of coffee while enjoying the beautiful beach view from under the shade of macadamia trees. Don't forget to try their macadamia ice cream on a hot day! We also highly recommend their macadamia crumb packs, which we used to coat our fresh fish.

Camp
Te Kaha Holiday Park: Basic facilities but a great location.

Maraehako Camp Ground: A popular locally run campground with lovely beachside camping.

Freedom camp
The Hoani Waititi Memorial Reserve is at Omaio, just beyond the Mōtū River mouth, and has a large freedom camping area. If you don't have water with you, get some drinking water at the Omaio General Store, as the reserve does not have drinking water on site.

Mōtū Rest Area: On the Mōtū Falls Rd, near the Whinray Scenic Reserve Track, this peaceful site is said to have kiwi around at night.

Gisborne/Te Tairāwhiti

This sunny region is a perfect destination to enjoy the salty air. Located in the eastern corner of the North Island, the tranquil coastal city of Gisborne offers a peaceful escape for those seeking beautiful beaches and great camping opportunities. You can also explore the small neighbouring towns and peninsulas, where you'll find many hidden gems waiting to be discovered.

East Cape

State Highway 35 around the East Cape is a stunning coastal drive that showcases many beautiful bays and small towns, in an area almost untouched by commercialisation. From Ōpōtiki to Te Araroa, the rugged, winding coastline opens up to gorgeous fishing bays, bush trails and friendly locals who enjoy beach life with bonfires, hunting and horses that roam freely. On the eastern side of the cape the road winds more inland, touching on a series of beautiful beaches.

I spent much of my childhood here, as this area is where my iwi is from: Te Whānau-ā-Apanui. You will even drive past my marae at Pōtaka, near Hicks Bay. This coastline is special and welcomes many campers with its wild beaches, perfect for surfcasting and soaking up the quiet, untouched landscapes.

Stock up on supplies and fuel in Ōpōtiki before you head off, because shops are few and far between along this route.

Camp
Island View Holiday Park: A classic Kiwi holiday park, just west of Ōpōtiki.

Tirohanga Beach Holiday Park: Dedicated to old-school camping, with shady campsites and easy access to the Dunes Trail cycleway.

Freedom Camp
Te Ahiaua Reserve: On State Highway 2, between Ōhiwa and Ōpōtiki, adorned with pōhutukawa. Locals call it the pipi bed. Sleep listening to the ocean. Must be self-contained.

Hikuwai Beach: About 3 km to the east of Ōpōtiki, at the start of State Highway 35. The campsite is nestled between the Dunes Trail and regenerating coastal bush, and is relatively small.

State Highway 35

While travelling towards Gisborne, you can discover many hidden gems. You will see marae with hand-carved wharenui and learn about the Māori history throughout the region, as well as enjoying the dramatic landscape and beautiful beaches on the eastern side of the cape.

Explore
Some highlights, travelling west to east:

- Visit the seaside Christ Church at Raukokore, which dates back to 1894, just before Waihau Bay, where you'll recognise the Waihau Bay Store from the movie *Boy*. It's a great place to stop, stay and fish.
- Cape Runaway: The eastern edge of the Bay of Plenty. You can't reach the cape itself by road, but there is a good beach and fishing at Whangaparāoa.
- Lottin Point: Divers flock here to enjoy the kaimoana and marine life. Stay at the Lottin Point Motel.
- Hicks Bay/Wharekahika: See the sun rise on the new day and explore this bay, with bush walks and waterfalls.

- Te Araroa: Visit the largest pōhutukawa tree in the world, Te Waha o Rerekohu.
- Te Puia Springs: Guests at the historic hotel can enjoy the natural mineral pool.
- Tokomaru Bay: A large beach and good fishing.
- Tolaga Bay: Walk the length of the historic wharf, or over the hill on the Cooks Cove Walkway, a scenic 6 km return route leading to a bay where Captain James Cook met with local Māori in 1769, including Te Kotere o te Whenua, a historic rock arch.

Experience

Maunga Hikurangi is a sacred mountain for the Ngāti Porou people, and you can experience it on a guided tour.
Te Urunga-Tu, the Sunrise Experience, is an unforgettable way to greet the dawn.

Camp

Anaura Bay Motor Camp: This beach is known for its pristine golden sand and crystal-clear water, making it an ideal spot for swimming, sunbathing and other water fun with the fam. Pull up a chair at the end of the day and enjoy the sound of the waves.

Tatapouri Bay Oceanside Accommodation: Locally owned and operated, this campground with a range of accommodation options sits on an amazing beach, not far from Gisborne.

Freedom camp

Tokomaru Bay: Freedom camping on the oceanfront. Must be self-contained.

Gisborne

Gisborne is the first city in the world to be greeted by the dawn each day. Its stunning beaches make for an ideal destination for explorers, sun-lovers and keen surfers. Gisborne is also a treasure trove of Māori culture, and you can learn more about the area's history at its excellent museum.

Experience
Gisborne is a show-off when it comes to pretty beaches and great surf spots. Midway Beach, Makorori, Tolaga Bay and Wainui Beach are a few hot spots to enjoy the sand between your toes, so have the surfboard waxed and hit those waves.

It's also renowned for being the unofficial 'Chardonnay capital of New Zealand'. Gisborne is the third-largest wine-producing region in New Zealand, and you can follow an impressive wine trail that leads to several boutique wineries.

Explore
Immerse yourself in the crystal-clear waters of Te Tapuwae o Rongokako Marine Reserve, north of the city. You will be amazed by the abundance of fascinating marine life living among the rock pools and shallow waters. A great way to spend the day with the kids.

Hidden gem
Nestled just 40 minutes northwest of Gisborne, the Rere Rockslide is an exciting adventure destination for older kids and adults. This impressive natural rockslide provides an exhilarating ride on a boogie board.

Freedom camp
Kaiti Beach: On the beach, over the river from the town.

Makorori Beach: A beautiful freedom campsite that boasts stunning sunsets and is perfect for surfing and swimming.

Hawke's Bay/Te Matau-a-Māui

The Hawke's Bay region is a beautiful part of the country, and has lots on offer if you are a wine enthusiast or are looking for a historic experience. I spent many school holidays here visiting my dad — I loved how it always felt like summer, and the stone fruit just tasted better than anywhere else!

Napier is world famous as an Art Deco city, full of character and beautiful architecture dating back to the 1930s, when it was reconstructed following the devastating 1931 earthquake.

Hawke's Bay is widely loved for its wine, boasting over 70 wineries to indulge in and explore. This region is also a horticultural paradise, producing abundant fruit and veges.

Māhia

The Māhia Peninsula has been a beloved vacation spot for generations of New Zealanders and visitors alike. The rugged coastline and wild waves make it a popular destination for fishing, boating and other water activities.

Explore
Mahanga Beach is a beautiful stretch of white sand north of the peninsula, on the eastern coast. You may even be able to spot seals or dolphins in the water.

Camp
Māhia Beach Motel and Holiday Park: Right on the beach. Nearby, the Mokatahi Hill Lookout offers breathtaking views of the surrounding coast and hills. The on-site Funky Fish cafe serves coffee, fresh food and real-fruit ice cream.

Te Urewera

Wairoa, south of Māhia on the way to Napier, is the gateway to Te Urewera, a huge and largely untouched forest region. You can hike, hunt or fish in the park, which is recognised as a living person and managed by local iwi Tūhoe.

Wairoa is the best place to stock up on supplies before heading into Te Urewera, on a road which has unsealed sections. Make a visit to the museum for an insight into the district's Māori and European history.

Camp
Waikaremoana Holiday Park: Powered and non-powered sites and cabins. Situated on Lake Waikaremoana, it's a perfect base for walks, fishing and relaxation in a stunning setting. Mobile coverage is limited, and the road is narrow, winding and unsealed in parts.

Napier/Hastings

Explore
Napier is known for its vibrant retro architecture, which attracts the attention of many visitors, who admire the colourful 1930s buildings scattered throughout the city. One of the most iconic heritage-listed buildings is the National Tobacco Company Building in Ahuriri, which was constructed in 1933.

The Esplanade at Westshore is a beautiful picnic area with spacious parking. Enjoy a lovely afternoon while watching the activity at the port and marina.

Tangoio Beach, north of Napier, is a beautiful stretch of beach, popular with locals. Grab a fresh-fruit ice cream and roll out the picnic rug.

Experience
Visit Ocean Spa for a relaxing and rejuvenating experience on the Napier waterfront. It offers ocean views from

its range of pools and spas, including a toddler pool and therapeutic pool with fountains and jets.

To get amongst the vineyards, you can take a bespoke wine tour, go by bike, or taxi from place to place. I recommend visiting the following wineries:

- Church Road: The winery features a large, lush lawn, and offers expert-led wine-tasting sessions.
- Mission Estate: With a historic dining room, this winery is a must-visit.
- Black Barn: Located in a natural amphitheatre, with a divine restaurant for those who are willing to splurge.
- Craggy Range: This winery offers exceptional wine, architecture, scenery and food.

Kids

Splash Planet amusement park in Hastings is the largest water park in New Zealand. There are activities for everyone; as well as pools and slides, visitors can enjoy mini-golf, the Fantasyland Express train, electric go-karts, beach volleyball and bumper boats. There are plenty of food options, and shaded tables where you can relax.

Eat

Taste of Summer in Bay View offers a variety of fresh fruits and vegetables — we were particularly drawn to their delicious fresh-fruit ice cream.

Funbuns in Hastings is a tastebud party! Its kitschy décor is funky and fun for the whole family. We loved the dumplings.

Camp

Kennedy Park Resort: Close to the heart of Napier and offering peaceful, park-like grounds. We enjoyed the excellent facilities, including a kids' library and a gym.

Hastings TOP 10 Holiday Park: Plenty of space to spread out, relax and play. Enjoy private spa pools, an outdoor swimming pool, landscaped grounds and a lake. From here you can easily access Napier and Havelock North by car.

Waipatiki Beach Holiday Park: On the coast north of Napier, nestled in its own little valley, you'll feel like you're a world away.

Havelock North

Havelock North is a place where you can discover some amazing farming, from fig orchards to honey bees, and of course, vineyards. The village is charming, too.

Explore
Te Mata Peak is a highlight of Hawke's Bay. It feels like you're off the beaten path until you hit the peak and uncover the beautiful view that you share with so many others taking in the end of the day. This park is also home to many wonderful walks and a restaurant. The upper part of the park has always been significant to the Māori culture. The area has been a site of human settlement for centuries, with fortified settlements, earthworks, and moa bones discovered in the region.

Hidden gem
The Maraetotara Falls, 15 minutes' drive outside Havelock North, has a picturesque waterfall and pools to cool off in.

Eat
Mamacita takes advantage of the local ingredients in the area to provide an authentic Mexican dining experience. A must-try dish is the costillas de cerdo.

Pipi Café: Full of charisma and the smell is gorgeous! Enjoy a delicious and authentic Neapolitan-style pizza.

Camp
The Village Pump House campground: Tucked away on the outskirts of the town, with loads of space to stretch out.

Taranaki

The Taranaki region is a coastal paradise that is renowned for its sunny days and stunning landscapes, with Taranaki Maunga, the second-highest peak in the North Island, rising in its centre. With its clear blue skies and pristine beaches, this area is an ideal escape for nature-lovers and adventure-seekers.

The crown jewel of the region is Mount Taranaki, a majestic peak that dominates the skyline. The mountain is surrounded by lush alpine rainforests which are home to a range of native flora and fauna. The area is a hiker's paradise, with numerous trails of varying difficulty that offer breathtaking views of the mountain and its surroundings.

Taranaki

Explore

My children were fascinated by the shimmering moss and bird melodies as we walked through the 'goblin forest' on the Kamahi Loop Track, on the eastern side of the mountain. The forest of kāmahi trees have grown in interesting layers, which my children believed would be amazing Peter Pan-style treehouses.

You can also walk through goblin forest to Wilkies Pools, a breathtaking series of naturally formed plunge pools. The crystal-clear water and stunning rock formations make for a beautiful and serene setting. Although the water can be quite chilly, even during the summer months, it's worth taking a dip amid the lush vegetation.

Another good walk on this side of the mountain leads to Curtis Falls, near Ngāti Ruanui Stratford Mountain House.

The Whitecliffs Walkway leads you on an incredible hike across sheer cliffs and bluffs. The dramatic white cliffs of Paraninihi are a sight to behold. North of Taranaki, the Three Sisters rock formations near the mouth of the Tongapōrutu River are another natural wonder.

During summer evenings, Pukekura Park in central New Plymouth is illuminated by a mesmerising Festival of Lights. This event, which first began in 1993, offers a nightly programme of music and performances amidst the park's lakes and lawns, creating a stunning spectacle of colourful lights.

Whitebaiting is a popular activity during the spring season. Taranaki's Waiwhakaiho River mouth is a busy spot for whitebaiting, with many enthusiasts lining its banks.

Experience

Explore the wonderful attraction of the heritage Forgotten World Highway, officially State Highway 43, from Taumarunui to Stratford. This scenic drive passes through isolated rural landscapes, charming towns and peculiar attractions.

The Govett-Brewster Art Gallery and Len Lye Centre is wonderful for families learning on the road and great for anyone on a rainy day.

Discover Taranaki's rich history through thousands of life-size models and scale figures at Tawhiti Museum in Hāwera. Experience the Traders and Whalers expedition, and go for a ride on the Tawhiti Bush Railway.

Hidden gem

The Hillsborough Holden Museum, a 15-minute drive from central New Plymouth, has the largest collection of Holden cars and memorabilia in the country. There's also a mini-golf course and a luge.

Eat

Bleached Coffee & Company in downtown New Plymouth entices with its sunny yellow décor, the aroma of fresh coffee and artisanal bagels.

Browse the Crystal Cylinder showroom while waiting for your hot flat white.

Camp

Seaview Holiday Park: This family-friendly spot is situated on the beachfront, in a prime location between the Awakino and Mōkau river mouths on the north Taranaki coast. Stunning views of Mount Taranaki and breathtaking sunsets.

Urenui Beach Camp: Another fantastic spot to enjoy the coast. Family-friendly with wide-open spaces.

Freedom camp

Lake Rotomanu, New Plymouth: Four marked spaces for non-self-contained freedom camping.

Battiscombe Terrace, Waitara: Six marked spaces, right on the oceanfront.

Surf Highway 45

Surfers: Taranaki is a dream destination. Surf Highway 45 offers some of the best surf breaks in the world, with waves that are perfect for beginners and experts alike.

We were told about Ōkato Graveyards, Rocky Lefts and Rocky Rights, as well as the better known Kumera Patch and Stent Road. These spots offer some of the best surfing experiences in New Zealand.

Ōakura is a charming village located along the Surf Highway, with an iconic black beach and gentle, rolling beach break which is great for kids who are learning to catch a wave.

Further south, it's worth doing the Ōpunakē Loop Trail, a 7 km stretch that offers great views of the lake, coast and countryside. Kids can explore the town by following the mural trail, ending the day with a delicious ice cream from the local dairy. The town's crescent-shaped beach is bustling with life in the summer months and is perfect for beginner surfers, thanks to its right- and left-handers.

There are also plenty of camp spots along the coast where you can pull in and enjoy the sound of the waves crashing on the shore. Watch the magical west-coast sunset in the evenings, as the sun dips below the horizon, casting a warm glow over the sea.

Manawatū-Whanganui

The Manawatū-Whanganui region, in the southern part of the North Island, has two main cities: Palmerston North and Whanganui. Both have a rich history, a vibrant arts scene and breathtaking scenic walks nearby.

Campers can enjoy many outdoor activities such as relaxing on quiet beaches, and hiking or cycling in the nearby Ruahine Range or Te Āpiti-Manawatū Gorge.

Tongariro National Park

My first snow adventure was a school trip to Mount Ruapehu. The bus was full of students all bundled up in puffer jackets, resembling Michelin men. We hit the slopes, made snow angels and had toboggan races. These memories are strong and have made me a believer in trying new things.

Ruapehu is still a great place for beginners or anyone who hasn't hit the slopes in a while. You can hire all the necessary equipment, including warm clothing, boots, goggles and helmets. It's also a good idea to book a lesson with a qualified ski or snowboard instructor, especially if it's your first time on the mountain.

Ruapehu's two ski areas offer a wide range of runs suitable for all skill levels, from beginner to advanced.

Explore
While skiing and snowboarding are fun activities, there are plenty of other things to do in the area. The Tongariro National Park offers breathtaking natural beauty and a range of walks and longer hikes.

Although the iconic Chateau hotel is now closed, its exterior and history are still worth admiring.

For families with small children, the Tawhai Falls Track near the Chateau takes you to the so-called Gollum Pool, where a scene from *The Lord of the Rings* was filmed. It's an easy and enjoyable walk. The Taranaki Falls and Soda Springs walks are also great options for those with older kids.

For more adventurous folk, the Tongariro Alpine Crossing or Tongariro Northern Circuit are both challenging and rewarding experiences.

Experience
Mount Ruapehu is home to New Zealand's largest commercial ski field, Whakapapa, on the northeastern side, and Tūroa on the south. You can have fun skiing, snowboarding, sledding and playing in the snow.

Camp
Tongariro Holiday Park: Just outside the northern edge of Tongariro National Park, the campsite provides a serene atmosphere with excellent amenities and stunning views of the surrounding bush and volcanoes.

Whakapapa Holiday Park: Conveniently located in the centre of the park, right next to the visitor centre. It is surrounded by alpine beech trees and a mountain stream runs through it.

Discovery Lodge: Offers rooms, campsites and shuttle services.

Freedom camp
Mangahuia DOC campsite: A basic camping site but centrally located. Spacious sites and you might hear kiwi at night.

Ohakune

During our trip to the area, we stayed in Ohakune, a charming town on the south side of Ruapehu. In ski season Ohakune is bustling with activity, with the Tūroa ski area located just a short shuttle ride up the mountain, and Whakapapa only an hour's drive away. Ohakune boasts the most vibrant après-ski scene in the region. This town also offers both summer and year-round activities, making it worth visiting and staying throughout the year.

Experience

Ohakune is an ideal destination for mountain-biking enthusiasts, with the stunning half-day Ohakune Old Coach Road being a popular starting point for the Mountains to Sea cycle trail. This ride takes several days and covers over 200 km, ending at Whanganui and the Tasman Sea.

In nearby Whanganui National Park, operators offer canoe trips and jet-boat tours to the famous Bridge to Nowhere.

Camp

Ohakune TOP 10 Holiday Park: This highly rated campground is surrounded by beautiful bushland, right on a mountain stream. We particularly enjoyed the parents' bathroom, and the riverside campsite.

Palmerston North

Palmerston North is often referred to as 'Palmy', and it is a small city with a big heart. In recent years, it has become a trendier town with lovely palm trees, great coffee shops and laid-back locals.

Explore

Te Motu o Poutoa/ANZAC Park, also known as Pork Chop Hill by locals, is a beautiful place to take a stroll and appreciate the scenery. Te Arapiki a Tāne, also called the Stairway of Tāne, is a great walk for families, although it is steep. The walk begins at the cliffside reserve and ends by the Manawatū River, consisting of almost 600 stairs in total. A cheeky lolly bag motivates the kids!

Te Āpiti-Manawatū Gorge is a stunning nature spot between the Manawatū and Wairarapa. There are fantastic views of the Manawatū River and the rocky gorge from walking and biking tracks and picnic areas.

He Ara Kotahi is a pathway that connects the city to Linton Military Camp and Massey University. It's a great way to explore the natural and cultural history of the region. The new bridge at Victoria Esplanade, which was designed to look like a fallen karaka tree, is absolutely stunning, and provides access to some amazing sights and sounds. As you walk or bike along the pathway you can spot some interesting wildlife such as kārearea, pheasants and herons. Take the time to read the information plaques along the way.

Experience

Wildbase Recovery is a great place to learn about New Zealand's native wildlife. Kākā, tūī, korimako, red-crowned kākāriki, tuatara, whio and pāteke are all residents here, being cared for and rehabilitated.

Kids

Victoria Esplanade is a beautiful and expansive green space that adds vibrancy to the entire city. It spans across 26 hectares and features bush walks, gardens and family-friendly activities. What made our visit even better was the bike track with clear road markings, which helped our kids learn bike safety.

Eat

Mouthwater Coffee Company has distinctive red coffee carts located in three central areas: Tremaine Ave, Main St and Cambridge Ave in Ashhurst. They are easy to spot and you can count on them for a great flat white.

There's nothing like picking up a hearty and tasty burger slung out of street caravan The Crafted and Co. Everything is made from scratch and their beef burger is unmatched. Don't run off too quickly — stay for dessert and grab a donut or one of the cookies they call 'mellow sammies'.

Camp

Ross' Campsite: A lovely atmosphere and great amenities on a family-run lifestyle block.

Himatangi Beach TOP 10 Holiday Park: Located 30 minutes outside of Palmerston North, this park offers a beautiful spot on the beach to enjoy a stunning west-coast sunset, along with all the top-notch facilities that come with a TOP 10 park.

Freedom camp

Woodville Ferry Reserve: A tranquil and beautiful place to camp or even just have a picnic. It is located by the Manawatū River, near Ballance Bridge. The reserve has basic facilities and a small wetland area — perfect to explore and observe local wildlife.

Whanganui

In 2021, Whanganui became the only UNESCO City of Design in New Zealand. As soon as I arrived, I was struck by the abundance of stunning architecture that surrounded me. There are several noteworthy buildings that are definitely worth admiring, as well as the Sarjeant art gallery, the Whanganui Regional Museum and many beautiful parks and gardens.

Explore

St Paul's Memorial Church in Pūtiki, over the river from the township, is a tribute to the Anglican mission's history in the area. Consecrated in 1937, the church's interior is of particular significance, showcasing revived Māori traditions fused with European neo-Gothic architecture.

The Sarjeant Gallery Te Whare o Rehua Whanganui is an architectural marvel which has been undergoing renovation and expansion, and is scheduled to reopen in late 2024.

The retro Embassy 3 cinema is another attraction that caught our eye, and what's cool is that it is still operating.

Article, in the old *Wanganui Chronicle* building, is a vibrant and colourful cafe that is always bustling with coffee lovers. From here, you can make your way to Moutoa Gardens near the river, a beautiful and serene spot.

Experience
A quick Google search will tell you about the most authentic river experience on Te Awa Tupua Whanganui River: the paddle steamer *Waimarie*. It's famous as the last remaining coal-fired paddle steamer from the golden era of riverboats in the late nineteenth and early twentieth centuries. You can enjoy an unforgettable experience learning about the region's heritage by taking a ride on this steamer and at the Riverboat Museum.

Eat
Experience the true taste of Mexico at La Quattro, located in the heart of Victoria Ave's bridge block. Traditional Mexican cuisine that will tantalise your taste buds.

Unwind and enjoy some delicious drinks after a long day at Maria Lane. Aim to be there for happy hour, when you can enjoy discounted drinks and a relaxed atmosphere.

At Lads Brewing Company you can discover a wide variety of flavourful craft beers, whether you're a beer enthusiast or just looking to try something new.

Frank Bar + Eatery is a cosy spot offering a great selection of cocktails and tasty bites.

Kids
The Kowhai Park playground, on the eastern bank of the river, has been entertaining children for decades. It features a brontosaurus for dinosaur enthusiasts and a pirate ship for those who love to imagine themselves sailing the high seas. Kids can also enjoy a ride on the Tot Town Railway during weekends and holidays.

Camp
Whanganui River TOP 10 Holiday Park: Enjoy the beautiful bird sanctuary and relax in the rec room, while kids can have fun at the pool, jumping pillow or playground, or bike around.

Whanganui Seaside Holiday Park: Located by Castlecliff Beach and perfect for fishing enthusiasts. You can either cast your line from the shore or launch your boat from the nearby ramp. The park offers great ocean views and easy access to both water- and land-based activities.

Lakelands Holiday Park: Discover this hidden gem on the banks of Lake Wiritoa, just off State Highway 3. Great views and abundant recreational activities.

Kai Iwi Beach Holiday Park: We fitted in well here with our '60s setup! This is a serene getaway nestled in a park-like setting, which offers easy access to fishing, long walks on soft iron sand, and exploration of the Kai Iwi cliffs.

Freedom camp

Moutoa Quay: A popular camping spot, but not available on Fridays due to the Saturday morning markets held there.

Kowhai Park: Easy place to stop for the night.

Taupo Quay, between Wilson St and Heads Rd: Centrally located campsite.

Wellington/Te Whanganui-a-Tara

The capital city and its surrounding areas are vibrant and diverse, featuring an overload of delightful small towns that are perfect for exploration. If you enjoy camping, Porirua, Lower Hutt and Upper Hutt are excellent choices for a short drive. On the stunning west coast of the North Island, Wairarapa is an area that I adore, with great wine and food. The nearby Kāpiti Coast boasts a lovely esplanade and friendly locals who are down to earth.

Wairarapa

Take a roadie for the day and head over to the Wairarapa. This region is where pinot noir first took root in New Zealand, and where some of the country's oldest vines still stand tall today. This is a magical place where you are invited to slow down and savour every sip of wine, as you wander among the vines and enjoy the spectacular scenery.

Explore

Nestled within the picturesque Wairarapa wine country lies the charming village of Martinborough. Take a wine tour or enjoy the pretty township with its tree-lined square.

Wairarapa is renowned not only for its wine but also for its cheese. One of the best cheese shops in the country, C'est Cheese, is located in the small town of Featherston. Housed in one of the town's oldest buildings, which is almost 150 years old, the shop boasts a cheese bar that serves heavily-cheesed scones.

Masterton is the largest town in the Wairarapa region, and is extremely family-friendly. It holds a special place in my heart, as my grandfather was a builder here in the 1960s. One of the main attractions in Masterton is Queen Elizabeth Park, which boasts one of the best children's playgrounds in New Zealand. The park offers a variety of activities such as a flying fox, paddle boats, bike rentals, miniature train, skate park, swing bridge and a mini-golf course.

One of the most popular spots on the Wairarapa coast is the Castlepoint lighthouse. The views from the lookouts are stunning.

On the southern coast, drive out to the Cape Palliser lighthouse and visit the nearby seal colony to see these cute creatures in their natural home.

Camp

Lake Domain Reserve: A private slice of paradise, on Lake Wairarapa south of Featherston.

Wairarapa Lake Shore Scenic Reserve: Another beautiful grassy camping spot that offers uninterrupted views of the lake.

Pūtangirua Pinnacles DOC campsite: A peaceful view of Cook Strait and a pretty, pebbly beach right by the Pūtangirua Stream.

Castlepoint Holiday Park: Enjoy a memorable stay in this stunning locality, with the lighthouse illuminated at night.

Kāpiti Coast/Paraparaumu

After camping in the South Island during winter, sometimes in the snow, we arrived at Kāpiti and were pleased to see the sun and beach. Kāpiti is a 40 km stretch of coastline with gorgeous open beaches, beautiful cliffs and rolling hills inland. One of the attractions of the area is its warmer climate — the temperature is usually a few degrees higher than in nearby Wellington. We loved Kāpiti's charm, happy atmosphere and abundance of outdoor activities.

Explore
The Escarpment Track provides lovely views of the coastline and Kāpiti Island, running from Paekākāriki to Pukerua Bay. It's a two-way trail, but most go from north to south. Families can enjoy this trail, but it's not for the faint-hearted, involving around 1200 steps, narrow pathways and two swing bridges.

Experience
Kāpiti Island Nature Reserve is a beautiful destination. However, to preserve its fragile ecosystem, the number of visitors is limited each day. The island is home to a variety of New Zealand native bird species, including takahē, kōkako and kākā. Access to the reserve is only through licensed tour operators.

We couldn't help but stop at the Southward Car Museum, after many locals had recommended it.

Kids
Kāpiti's Maclean Park is an ideal family destination with beachside access, a marine-themed playground, public facilities, a large skate park, basketball hoop and ample picnic spots. It is near lots of cute coastal cafés and restaurants and rows of camper carparks.

Eat
A cosy espresso bar called The Roastery, located in an industrial garage on Sheffield St in Paraparaumu, serves expertly brewed coffee and local pies and other treats. As we sipped our piccolos, the kids had a blast playing ping pong.

Down the street is the famous Tuatara Brewery and Tap Room. Enjoy a tasting paddle outside under the umbrellas. This street is bustling, with a donut truck and Duncan's Brewing Company just down the road.

Camp
El Rancho: A beautiful family holiday park on the Waikanae River, only a short walk away from Waikanae Beach. The park offers a wide range of amenities, including comfortable accommodation, a swimming pool, a playground and barbecue facilities.

Paekakariki Holiday Park: Lovely sites available under pōhutukawa trees.

Freedom camp
Waikanae Estuary: Watch locals netting for whitebait, enjoy scenic walks, take in the sunset on the beach and even find secret swimming holes nearby.

Ōtaki Beach: On the banks of the Ōtaki River. Only six spaces. Must be self-contained.

Wellington

Wellington, despite its reputation as a windy place, is a true gem that offers so much more than just a gateway to the south. Spend some time here and you will discover a hub of culture that is home to a plethora of attractions and activities.

For those who love a challenge, the hilly climbs around the city will provide a great workout and stunning views. Mount Victoria is a must-visit attraction, with its panoramic views of the city and surrounding hills.

Take your time to explore Wellington and its surroundings, and you'll discover a truly special place that is full of surprises. If you have an interest in food, you will be satisfied with the exceptional seafood and other treats provided at the eateries located on the waterfront. There is no shortage of things to do in Wellington for those who appreciate a hip urban atmosphere, with attractions ranging from street art and live music venues to fashionable bars.

Whenever I reminisce about my time as a flight attendant and staying overnight in Wellington, the fragrant smell of coffee comes to mind. I believe my selective coffee habits stem from the 5 a.m. flights I used to take from here, where I would order a Mojo coffee at the airport to wake me up.

Beyond Wellington, nearby areas are equally charming and full of charisma. The Wairarapa (see page 174) and Kāpiti Coast (see page 176) are a couple of my favourites, each with their own special charm and natural beauty.

Explore

Mount Victoria is one of the most popular attractions in Wellington, providing stunning views of the city and beyond. The summit is located on Lookout Rd and it is easily accessible. There are also walking and biking trails in the area that offer an opportunity to explore and enjoy the fresh air.

Experience

Discover the hidden beauty of Wellington by taking a ride on the Cable Car, which began running in 1902. It was an instant success, with over 425,000 passengers taking the ride in the first year. The Cable Car takes you on a short five-minute ride from the city centre through the terraced houses of Kelburn on the hillside, then brings you to the lookout point high above the city. From here, you can visit the Botanic Garden, the Cable Car Museum and Space Place at the Carter Observatory.

Immerse yourself in the rich and diverse natural environment, delve into Māori culture, explore captivating art and unravel the fascinating history of New Zealand at the state-of-the-art Museum of New Zealand Te Papa Tongarewa. With its innovative exhibits, interactive displays and immersive storytelling, Te Papa offers an unforgettable experience that celebrates the best of New Zealand's past, present and future.

If you're a *Lord of the Rings* fan who wants to delve deeper into the movie's production and learn the secrets behind the making of the special effects, costumes and props, then Wētā Workshop is the perfect place for you. You'll get a close-up perspective on the creative process, taking you through every stage from initial concept to the finished product.

Kids

Wellington Zoo was the first zoo in New Zealand, and has been caring for animals since 1906. It's a great place to spend a day with the family, with plenty of fun and interactive talks. Kids can get close to farm animals at the Meet the Locals He Tuku Aroha exhibit and explore the various playgrounds.

Eat

The Wellington waterfront is a vibrant area, with large numbers of bustling cafes and restaurants, street art to admire and a pier for fishing. Our family decided to have dinner at The Crab Shack, which was family-friendly and a clear favourite among the many patrons who were enjoying the lively atmosphere.

Take a stroll around the city and you will come across Mojo Coffee. It's a local-favourite chain that serves some of the best coffee in town.

Camp

Wellington TOP 10 Holiday Park, Lower Hutt: These spacious grounds are located approximately 15 km away from the Wellington city centre. A good place to stay before catching the ferry or as a base to explore Wellington.

Freedom camp

Evans Bay Marina carpark: Clean toilets and easy parking. However, due to the limited parking space, leave your van to hold your space and catch a bus or taxi into Wellington.

Crossing Cook Strait

Travelling between New Zealand's North and South Islands is a breathtaking experience in itself, with mesmerising scenery that will leave you spellbound. It is a comfortable journey with plenty of seating, a bar, restaurant and gift shops, and playgrounds.

Each ship is different, but both ferry services (Interislander and Bluebridge) cater to passengers, cars, motorhomes and caravans.

With two operators and multiple sailings daily, you'll have ample time to cross. It is best to plan your crossing in advance, as the ferries do tend to book out quickly, especially if you are towing a caravan. Weather can affect sailings and cause cancellations.

Discounts are available for Interislander bookings through Tasman Holiday Parks and the NZMCA.

Marlborough/Te Tauihu-o-te-Waka

Marlborough is such a beautiful and unforgettable region. Enter through Picton and take in the beautiful sounds. The area is known for its temperate climate, which is favoured by wine-makers — the region has gained recognition worldwide for its delightful Sauvignon Blanc. Discover vibrant and peaceful towns that offer stunning scenery and wonderful camping. You can indulge in water activities, such as diving and fishing, and enjoy the delicious seafood on offer. Nature enthusiasts can revel in Marlborough's diverse landscape, which ranges from charming vineyards nestled in valleys to the protected waterways of Marlborough Sounds.

Marlborough Sounds

Arriving on the ferry in Picton, you'll be greeted by a charming coastal town that serves as the gateway to the Marlborough Sounds. It's a place where I feel completely calm — the water is glassy and the wine is divine.

The complex network of waterways presents wonderful opportunities to enjoy activities on the water, such as leisurely cruising and observing wildlife. You can also venture into regenerating forest.

Picton has a grassy and busy seafront, including a pirate playground, with lovely restaurants and cafes behind. The floating maritime museum and aquarium are great for families, and the Queen Charlotte Track is a popular scenic hiking or biking experience.

Explore

Queen Charlotte Sound is a paradise of island sanctuaries and pristine waters, where native birdlife thrives. You can also enjoy delicious food at resorts and restaurants tucked away in the beautiful bays bordered by native bush. Explore the area with kayak rentals or yacht charters.

The Tirohanga Track takes you through native bush to a viewpoint that offers amazing views of Picton, Waikawa and the Marlborough Sounds. It's a bit of a climb, but it's worth it.

Experience

Pelorus Eco Adventures offers great kayaking tours for families with younger children. You can enjoy the picturesque Pelorus River and experience the magic of the *Hobbit* movies as you pass iconic spots from the trilogy and learn insider information about the filming process.

Take a boat tour on the sounds — there are various operators offering scenic, eco or dolphin-watching tours.

Taste your way around Marlborough Sounds, enjoying this seafood haven paired with the region's famous wines.

Eat

Before a tour or hopping on the ferry, grab a quick bite at Toastie Lords, overlooking the water and also serving great coffee. The Ivan (pastrami, sauerkraut and pickle) is my favourite.

Camp

Tasman Holiday Parks Picton: Camping doesn't come much more convenient, with sheltered sites in a tent village and large caravan sites, both powered and unpowered. There's an outdoor pool and spa, too.

Parklands Marina Holiday Park: Ideal for boating enthusiasts, situated close to Waikawa Bay, the marina and boat ramp. Fish-filleting station and barbecues in the courtyard.

Whatamango Bay DOC campsite: A pleasant bay in which to relax in peace.

Aussie Bay DOC campsite: Handy for kayaking and nearby walks.

Momorangi Bay DOC campground: Call this great spot home for a few days. Great facilities, jetty and playground, plus glowworms nearby.

Havelock

The drive from Picton to Havelock is a highly recommended road-trip adventure. To enjoy stunning views of the Queen Charlotte and Pelorus sounds, head along the Queen Charlotte Drive, which stretches for 34 km to Havelock. Don't forget to stop at the Cullen Point lookout.

You will notice numerous mussel farms in the sounds; this industry is significant here. Havelock is known as New Zealand's greenshell mussel capital, and is situated between the Pelorus and Kaituna rivers. It is a good place to stop when travelling to Picton from Nelson. Stop into Mills Bay Mussels to pick up some fresh-shucked protein gems.

This charming town also offers a wide range of water-based activities. At Havelock's marina, visitors can arrange water taxis, charter boats for fishing or touring the Pelorus and Kenepuru sounds, and sea kayaks for guided or self-guided paddling tours.

Hidden gem
French Pass is well off the beaten track. A scenic and winding road leads you to this beautiful, peaceful destination, where there is a DOC campsite.

Camp
Elaine Bay DOC campsite: A great base for exploring Pelorus Sound by boat, or walking or mountain-biking on nearby tracks. Enjoy views of emerald waters right from your campsite.

Blenheim

Surrounding the town of Blenheim are dramatic landscapes: high, dry hills and acres upon acres of grapevines on the valley floor. Stop in and explore vineyards that stretch out to the horizon. Take time to explore the vineyards and learn about the winemaking process, from the cultivation of grapes to the final product in the glass.

Blenheim is famous for its high levels of sunshine, and the surrounding mountains trap the summer heat. The town is bustling with activity, and visitors can choose from a variety of cafes and restaurants.

Explore
Spend the afternoon picnicking at the Taylor River Reserve, enjoying beautiful views while the kids play.

Experience
We'd better start with wine. The Marlborough region of New Zealand is renowned for its exceptional white wines, with over 150 wineries spread throughout the region, making it the largest wine-growing region in the country. Marlborough produces a wide balance of wine styles, from its famous clean and refreshing sauvignon blanc to elegant chardonnay and pinot gris. Take a tour with Hop n Grape, or make your

own way around. These are some of my favourites:

- Saint Clair is a family-run estate renowned for producing exceptional wines for over 30 years. Their vineyards span over 160 hectares of prime land in the Wairau and Awatere valleys. Knowledgeable staff will guide you through a curated selection of their award-winning wines, and as you sip, you can enjoy stunning views of the surrounding vineyards and mountains.
- As a former flight attendant who served Cloudy Bay in the sky, I know how highly regarded this winery is among wine lovers. Cloudy Bay was one of the first wineries in Marlborough and although I am not a sommelier, I must say that their Te Koko Marlborough Sauvignon Blanc is soft and delicious. I highly recommend visiting their cellar door.

The Moa Brewing Company has an impressive history of producing high-quality, multi-award-winning beers. For those who love beer and enjoy trying new flavours, Moa's Tap Room is a great place to visit.

Omaka Aviation Heritage Centre is a must-visit destination. This world-class centre showcases World War I history in an engaging and interactive way.

Eat

One of the highlights of Blenheim is the Marlborough Farmers' Market, which offers a tasty opportunity to purchase fresh produce directly from local growers and producers. It's on every Sunday morning at the A&P Showgrounds.

Hedgerows is a family-owned hydroponic strawberry farm located just five minutes from Blenheim. Buy fresh-fruit ice cream and berries from September to January.

If you're heading south of Blenheim along State Highway 63, Wairau Valley Tavern serves up the best pie I have had in the country. An old-school classic that melts in your mouth.

Camp

Spring Creek Holiday Park: Sitting pretty on the river. An evening pink sky makes it extra lovely.

Freedom camp

Taylor Dam Reserve: Lush trees and surroundings, easy lake access. Self-contained only.

Whites Bay DOC campsite: Grassy sites offer ample space and access to wonderful walks, including the Black Jack track, for stunning views.

Marfells Beach DOC campsite: South of Blenheim, off State Highway 1, this is a wonderful surprise spot with ocean views.

Wairau Diversion Reserve: A quiet location for self-contained vehicles, with sea views and onsite toilets.

Lansdowne Park: A lovely place with large sports fields. Camping Monday to Thursday only.

Green-lipped mussels in red sauce

Green-lipped mussels are a popular shellfish in New Zealand due to their abundance and high protein content. If you want to enjoy a delicious pot of mussels without having to gather them, they can be found in live water baths at almost every supermarket.

¼ cup olive oil
1 cup diced bacon
1 onion, finely chopped
3 garlic cloves, minced
salt, to taste
⅛ teaspoon freshly ground black pepper
1 cup red wine
bunch of fresh coriander, chopped
400 g (14 oz) can cherry tomatoes
¼ teaspoon dried thyme
1.5 kg (3 lb 5 oz) mussels, scrubbed and debearded
sourdough bread, to serve

Heat the olive oil in a large pot over medium heat. Add the diced bacon and cook until crispy, stirring occasionally.

Add the chopped onion and garlic, along with a seasoning of salt and pepper. Cook for 5 minutes or until the onion is translucent.

Add the wine, then the chopped coriander, cherry tomatoes and thyme. Stir well.

Add the mussels to the pot and stir gently. Allow to cook for 3–5 minutes or until they have all opened.

Serve with buttered bread, by the seaside.

Nelson Tasman/Whakatū

Nelson is a wonderful destination that offers something for everyone. Smaller towns like Golden Bay, Motueka and Kaiteriteri boast beautiful bays, saltwater baths and fantastic farmers' markets. Spend some time exploring these charming towns and taking in the stunning scenery. Nelson city is a hub of activity, with a wide range of fun-filled outdoor activities to enjoy. From hiking and mountain-biking to kayaking and paddleboarding, there's no shortage of adventure to be had.

Discover the turquoise waters of the Abel Tasman National Park, a beloved wilderness reserve with plenty of natural beauty to take in. The park draws in travellers from around the world, and is famous for its stunning beaches, scenic walks, breathtaking waterfalls and exciting water sports.

Nelson and surrounds

Explore

It's a must to check out the Nelson Market, on every Saturday morning. It's famous for its bustling atmosphere and the local artists, artisans, food vendors and other businesses that showcase their work there. There are also weekend markets in Motueka and Tākaka, the Nelson Farmers' Market on Wednesdays and a Twilight Market at Isel Park on Thursdays during the summer.

Take a picturesque walk from Cable Bay to Glenduan. The entire walk takes about 3.5 hours and starts at Cable Bay's historically significant shingle beach, offering amazing panoramic views of the Tasman Bay seascape. You can start at either end of the track but will need to arrange return transport from the far end. It's a workout but the rewards are definitely worth it.

Head inland to the Nelson Lakes National Park and take a peaceful walk around Lake Rotoiti, listening to the enchanting calls of native birds.

Discover the beauty of the Moutere Valley. Visit a few cellar doors, check out inspiring artisan stores and galleries, and enjoy fish and chips on the Māpua Wharf.

Experience

Take the famed Great Taste Trail, a cycling adventure that allows you to discover the best of what the region has to offer. Take on the whole 200 km loop over a few days or just take a bite of one of the sections of town or country riding.

If you are a peanut-butter lover like us, then Pic's Peanut Butter World will make you happy! Made in Nelson, Pic's is simply the best. It has no added ingredients, just pure peanuts, exactly how it should be. You can visit their factory and watch as the peanuts are roasted, churned and crushed, as well as seeing the world's biggest jar of peanut butter.

Tip

Our favourite way to eat peanut butter is in a wrap with banana and cinnamon, or bake it into a brownie (see page 196).

Eat

Urban Oyster Bar & Eatery in Nelson offers bold and creative flavours in a relaxed setting. Sit by the open kitchen and watch the chefs at work.

The Moutere Inn holds the distinction of being the oldest pub in the country to be housed in its original building. The pub's historic architecture and charming ambience make for an impressive place to relax and enjoy a pint of beer along with a delicious pub meal. What's even better is that The Moutere Inn welcomes self-contained campervans, making it a perfect spot for a relaxing stopover.

Camp

Tāhuna Beach Holiday Park: A peaceful retreat located close to Nelson city centre. Camp seaside and star-gaze into the night.

Mapua Leisure Park: Situated at the point where the tidal waters of the Waimea Estuary flow into Tasman Bay. (Just a note, in February and March the park is clothes optional, i.e. there are naturists holidaying there.)

Cable Bay Holiday Park: Powered and non-powered sites in a beautiful setting.

Freedom camp
There are several designated areas for freedom camping in Nelson, which require self-containment. These include:

- Isel Park (Main Road Stoke Carpark)
- Wakapuaka Reserve Carpark
- Maitai Cricket Ground Carpark
- Queen Elizabeth II Drive Gardens
- Trafalgar Park/Haven Foreshore (Kinzett Terrace Carpark)
- Buxton Square Carpark
- Montgomery Carpark (Monday to Thursday only).

Outside of Nelson, freedom camping areas include Motueka Beach Reserve and Alexander Bluff Road Reserve, Ngātīmoti.

Peanut-butter brownie

Whenever we have a camp dinner, I make my crowd-pleasing peanut-butter brownies. You can bake them in the oven if your caravan has one, over some coals in a pan with a lid or in a lidded barbecue.

1 cup plain flour
¾ cup dark cocoa
¾ cup brown sugar
1⅓ cups caster sugar
175 g (6 oz) unsalted butter, melted, plus extra for greasing
⅓ teaspoon salt
1 teaspoon vanilla extract
3 eggs
150 g (5½ oz) dark chocolate nibs (or chocolate drops)
½ cup crushed peanuts
⅓ cup smooth peanut butter

Mix the flour and cocoa in a bowl, then add the brown and caster sugars, melted butter, salt, vanilla and eggs. Combine to a smooth consistency. Fold in the chocolate nibs or drops and crushed peanuts, and swirl in spoonfuls of peanut butter.

To cook in a campfire, cut and lay buttered baking paper in your skillet on your trivet, then pour the batter over the baking paper and cover with a lid. Bake the brownie in the fire; have about 20 per cent of the coals underneath and pop 80 per cent on top. Cook for 45 minutes.

To cook in the oven, bake at 160°C (315°F) for 40–45 minutes.

Remove the brownie from the skillet carefully, pulling the baking paper up to lift it out, or remove from the oven. Divide it amongst your campers and enjoy warm, with ice cream.

Golden Bay

Golden Bay is a place that seems too good to be true. The sound of the sea adds tranquillity and soul to the area. I recently returned to celebrate my grandmother's eightieth birthday in her childhood home and couldn't help but wonder why she ever left. Everything is serene, peaceful and stunningly beautiful.

Golden Bay has a lot to offer aside from its sunshine and lovely beaches: kaimoana such as scallops, whitebait and other fish, lush farmlands and wonderful nature reserves. It's a major point of entry to the Abel Tasman National Park (see page 202), one of New Zealand's greatest tourist attractions.

Explore

Te Waikoropupū Springs are the largest cold-water springs in the Southern Hemisphere. The water is a bright emerald, with an impressive visual clarity of around 76 metres, making it some of the purest water in the world. The spring flows at an incredible rate of approximately 14,000 litres per second, and the bubbles emanating from it are a spectacle to behold. The springs are easily accessible via a flat walk under the canopy of mānuka and kānuka that takes around 20 minutes, along boardwalks and across bridges. You will be able to admire the beauty of the springs once you reach the viewing platform, but you can't swim in them.

Wharariki Beach, to the west of Farewell Spit, is simply mesmerising. We are committed sunset chasers, and here lies a beautiful place to take it all in. A short walk through coastal forest and rolling pastures will reveal a beach that's so vast you could easily explore it for days. As you wander along the coast you'll encounter an enchanting scattering of caves, rocks and arches that have been shaped entirely by the elements of the wild west coast. The rugged beauty of this place is truly breathtaking.

Camp

Pohara Beach TOP 10 Holiday Park: This park, on the coast near Tākaka, is an ideal base for exploring the natural beauty of Golden Bay, with uninterrupted beach access.

Golden Bay Holiday Park: Classic Kiwi campsite on the way to Farewell Spit.

Wharariki Beach Holiday Park: Explore the majestic beauty of Wharariki Beach and Farewell Spit in Golden Bay. This rugged and unspoilt coastline is one of New Zealand's most precious natural treasures, offering stunning views of the Tasman Sea and an array of wildlife. You can easily walk to the beach from the holiday park and immerse yourself in the natural wonder of this amazing location.

Takaka Camping and Cabins: Conveniently located close to the main township and around 30 minutes to the Abel Tasman National Park.

Canaan Downs DOC campsite: Off the beaten track, secluded and quiet.

Abel Tasman National Park

The Abel Tasman National Park is a prime destination for nature lovers and adventure seekers. An array of well-formed tracks weave through a breathtaking coastal environment, offering stunning views of bush and golden beaches. The 51 km track through the park can be easily broken up into smaller sections, allowing you to explore the park at your own pace. You can also make a day trip by choosing from a variety of tours offered by local operators, including water taxis, kayak tours and cruises.

During autumn, the park's scenery is particularly awe-inspiring, with the landscape turning a beautiful golden hue. The calm water conditions make it an excellent time to go on a kayak tour and explore the National Park's expansive golden coves and stretches of beaches.

The Abel Tasman National Park is the destination for those outdoor lovers looking for a memorable and adventurous day trip. With its stunning scenery, well-formed tracks, and a variety of tour options, it's easy to see why this park is a top-rated attraction.

Explore
We all love chasing waterfalls, and the Wainui Falls are particularly fun to discover. It's a moderate hike of around 1.5 hours return, so make sure to pack your lunch. Make your way through the native forest with plenty of places to take a breather, and an impressive swing bridge. You'll hear the falls before you see them.

Sometimes we need to recharge the batteries at the beach. Kaiteriteri, which is located just outside the national park, is one of New Zealand's best known and most beautiful beaches. The water is a stunning turquoise, and the golden sand is perfect for taking it slow and building sandcastles.

Experience
Abel Tasman Kayaks in Mārahau is one of the country's oldest and largest kayak-rental companies. They offer both guided tours and kayak hire so you can make your own adventure.

Camp
Tōtaranui DOC campground: Over 800 sites located across the road from the beach and the estuary.

The Barn Cabins & Camp: Under the mountains, on the mouth of the ocean, this is nature at its finest. Take a leisurely stroll to the beach and dig for pipis, or gaze up at the stars while toasting marshmallows in a private pit during the fire season. Be sure to try the delicious woodfired pizzas at The Park Café.

Bethany Park: On the Kaiteriteri inlet, with spacious and beautiful beaches. Walking distance to the beach.

Kaiteriteri Recreation Reserve: A vast campground located across the road from a beautiful golden beach. If you prefer a peaceful and spacious site, choose one under the trees. We enjoyed fresh tarakihi and chips from Gone Burgers.

Murchison

Heading south and inland from Nelson, the next destination on the journey is Murchison. Known as the whitewater capital of New Zealand, Murchison is famous for the thrilling whitewater rafting experiences that can be had on the Buller and Mātakitaki rivers. The rapids are guaranteed to get your adrenaline pumping, while the scenic beauty of the Maruia Falls is easy to access and enjoy.

Experience
Maruia Hot Springs offers a luxurious day spa and wellness experience. It is located within the scenic Lewis Pass Scenic Reserve, nestled among the snow-capped Southern Alps. You can also camp there overnight.

Hidden gem
Take a dip in the Buller River at the Eel Hole swimming spot near Murchison. You can also have a river swim in the Maitai, Lee and Aniseed valleys near Nelson, and the Aorere River in Golden Bay. Another local favorite is Paines Ford near Tākaka.

Camp
The Riverside Holiday Park is situated by the Buller River and boasts 16 hectares of beautiful grounds. It's only a 10-minute walk from Murchison township and is particularly popular among kayakers and rafters. Children can have fun on the playground and jumping pillow, and there's also a swimming hole for hot summer days.

Potato whitebait cakes

Tākaka has always produced excellent whitebait. While I lack experience in catching this New Zealand delicacy, I can share my recipe for them.

2 cups mashed potatoes
1 cup all-purpose flour
½ teaspoon ground black pepper
½ teaspoon salt
1 egg
1 cup whitebait
½ cup olive oil and a knob of butter, for frying
lemon slices, to serve

In a bowl, mix the mashed potatoes, flour, black pepper and salt until well combined.

Whisk the egg into the whitebait, then mix it into the potato mixture to make a batter.

Heat olive oil and butter in a skillet over medium heat.

Drop pan-sized circles of batter into the hot oil and cook until golden brown, about 4–5 minutes per side. Drain the fried patties on paper towels.

Serve with a slice of lemon.

West Coast/Te Tai Poutini

Embark on a journey like no other as you travel along the Great Coast Road between Westport and Greymouth, a route that has earned its place among the best road trips in the world. Prepare to be swept away by the breathtaking views of the vast ocean and the lush rainforest that surrounds you. The deep blue waters on one side and the verdant forest on the other create a stunning contrast that is hard to match.

Once you hit the road, you will be greeted with an abundance of natural wonders that will take your breath away. Coming from Nelson, you will begin your journey in Westport, a charming seaside town that dates back to 1861. Its goldrush history and heritage are evident in its architecture and landmarks.

Further south, the Glacier Highway (State Highway 6) will lead you from Greymouth through Hokitika then through the Franz Josef and Fox Glacier villages, before taking you to Haast, where the road heads inland and links through to Central Otago. Each of these places offers a different experience, from the rugged beauty of the glaciers to the quaint charm of Hokitika, where you can browse for pounamu (greenstone) and other local treasures.

West Coast

Explore

Take a leisurely walk through the lush beech and podocarp forest of the Kahurangi National Park while crossing limestone outcrops along a well-defined trail beside the Ōpārara River. You will eventually arrive at the magnificent Ōpārara limestone arch, which is believed to be the largest in Australasia and is estimated to be 35 million years old. This walk is ideal for families with children, as it is easy to navigate.

Punakaiki is a small town near to the breathtaking Paparoa National Park, popular for its remarkable landscape and the captivating Pancake Rocks and blowholes. The Pancake Rocks are a unique geological formation shaped over millions of years, which resemble stacks of pancakes. The blowholes are created when waves crash into the rock formations and create spectacular sprays of water that can reach over 20 metres in height. Observe these natural wonders from a safe distance on several viewing platforms.

Head inland and take a pleasant bush walk to the magnificent Coal Creek Falls, a refreshing spot for swimming during hot summer months.

Carters Beach near Westport is a popular spot for families, with a playground on the domain.

If you're into surfing, Tauranga Bay is a great place to go. It's known for its left-hand point and beach break, which are best during low tide and a 2-metre swell. To the south is Nine Mile Beach, which faces southwest and has some of the best beach breaks in the area when conditions are right.

Experience

UnderWorld Adventures, based in Charleston, will blow you away with their many wonderful tours, from underground rafting to glowworm cave tours and adventure caving, allowing you to explore the stunning underground world. Each tour provides a special experience and an opportunity to witness the beauty of the limestone country of the Paparoa National Park.

Camp

Punakaiki Beach Camp: A serene and picturesque camping experience. The camp boasts breathtaking views of the imposing limestone cliffs that loom over the site, creating an awe-inspiring backdrop for your stay. You can easily access the golden sandy beach within a minute's walk of the camp.

Carters Beach (Westport) TOP 10 Holiday Park: Carters Beach is a stunning location. Keep an eye out for the Dinosaur Tree, which is a hit with kids, and take some time to explore the Cape Foulwind seal colony nearby.

Westport Kiwi Holiday Park: A 10-minute stroll from the main street, its tranquil position provides a peaceful escape where guests can wake up to the sweet melodies of native birds.

Freedom camp
Freedom camping is widely spread throughout the Grey District, on council-controlled property for self-contained campers, although there are some areas where it is banned.

The park at Cargill Rd, Barrytown is right on the seafront.

Hidden gem
Gentle Annie Campground, located in Mokihinui north of Westport, is a serene enclave for nature enthusiasts and adventure-seekers. The area boasts pristine beaches, lush vegetation and rugged terrain, and the campground has an amazing site at the river mouth.

Greymouth

Greymouth is a charming town located at the mouth of the Grey River, and is the largest urban centre on the West Coast — the locals fondly call it the 'Big Smoke'. It's a popular place for locals to restock and refuel, while travellers find it an enticing gateway to numerous tramping trails.

Despite occasional dreary weather, Greymouth offers much more than meets the eye. The town has a rich goldmining history and is home to several pounamu (greenstone, jade) shops that showcase local artistry. The town's surroundings feature lots of notable walks and Monteith's Brewery, a popular local attraction, is known for its good Kiwi beer.

Explore
The Point Elizabeth Walkway offers a delightful trek along a water raceway constructed by miners during goldrushes of the nineteenth century. Enjoy breathtaking views of the mountain ranges inland and you may also spot the playful Hector's dolphins and New Zealand fur seals from the clifftop lookout. The walkway is also home to various native bird species, making it an excellent spot for birdwatching enthusiasts.

Experience
Check out the charming museum town of Shantytown, a fascinating time warp. Take a steam-train ride through the bush and try gold panning. Your children will be mesmerised by the sights and sounds of this delightful destination.

Eat
Head to Monteith's Brewery and savour a clean pale ale with local venison sausages.

Hidden gem
I highly recommend heading inland, from either Westport or Greymouth, and making a stop in Reefton, a charming town also known as the 'town of light', as it was the first place in New Zealand to have a public supply of electricity. You won't want to miss a visit to the renowned Reefton Distilling Co., where you can learn about the distillation process and sample some of their award-winning gin and other spirits. Afterward, take a leisurely

stroll down the town's main street and browse through the quaint shops, where you're sure to find some locally made treasures. As you wander through the town, you'll discover fascinating stories and landmarks that offer a glimpse into the town's past and the pioneering spirit of its people.

Camp
Greymouth Seaside TOP 10 Holiday Park: A wonderful place to stay, with exceptional facilities.

Freedom camp
Cobden/Aromahana Lagoon: Toilets and an outdoor shower. An easy beachfront space to park for the night.

Hokitika

The heart of the West Coast, Hokitika is a charming town that boasts natural wonders, authentic experiences and warm, welcoming locals. You can hike through the towering trees of the Hokitika Gorge, explore the wild beauty of Lake Kaniere, or simply soak in the stunning views of the Southern Alps and the wild coast.

Explore
I was amazed at how much more beautiful the Hokitika Gorge was 'in person' than in pictures. This natural wonder is easily accessible via a bush track, which leads to a breathtaking view of vibrant turquoise waters flowing through forest, surrounded by tall limestone cliffs as white as snow. The combination of colours is truly a sight to behold, making it a paradise for photographers.

Spend a peaceful afternoon exploring the stunning Hokitika Beach, which stretches along the breathtaking coastline that backs the township. The beach boasts smooth stones and driftwood scattered across its sandy shores. Enjoy a camp dinner as you watch the sun slowly dip into the ocean — there's no better way to end your day.

Mahināpua Walkway/Mananui Tramline: Take in the breathtaking landscape of Lake Mahināpua while walking or mountain-biking on an old logging tramline — perfect for the whole family. The track takes you through the heart of the lush and verdant forest, and one of the highlights is the boardwalk that takes you across the wetlands. The track is part of the West Coast Wilderness Trail cycle trail.

Experience
West Coast Treetop Walkway and Tower Zipline is an attraction suitable for the whole family. You can either walk among the treetops or climb over a hundred steps to the top of the spiral tower and hook up for a tandem zipline, flying through the rimu forest at speeds of over 60 km/hr.

Eat
Espresso Bar: Funky retro atmosphere, yummy bites and seriously good coffee.

Camp
Lake Mahināpua DOC campsite: Lovely

place to spend the night. Can be busy as it is an attractive space but there are lots of spots available. Good facilities.

Hans Bay DOC campsite, Lake Kaniere: Tucked 20 minutes away from Hokitika, this campsite has a jetty and boat-launch ramp. A brief stroll will take you to the Dorothy Falls, a multi-tiered waterfall with a pool at its base.

Hokitika Holiday Park: Great for families with young children to relax after a long day of exploring. The park features a pirate-themed playground with a flying fox. Kids can also enjoy running around freely, playing with the farm animals and spotting the roaming weka.

Ross Beach TOP 10 Holiday Park: 2 km south of Ross township, offering campsites and cool pod-style accommodation.

Freedom camp
The Treetop Walkway also offers spaces to spend the night, near the cafe.

Ōkārito

Ōkārito Lagoon, 130 km south of Hokitika and covering an area of approximately 12 sq km, is the largest unmodified wetland in all of New Zealand. Its water is so blue that it appears drinkable. You will be welcomed by the many pesky sandflies but also big smiles from the locals. This is a great place to completely detach and relax.

Explore
The Ōkārito area is a great place for bird-watching. One of the rarest birds found in the area is the kōtuku or white heron — its only breeding area in New Zealand is located very close to Ōkārito. Many other wading birds can also be seen in the area.

Beach it for the evening, enjoy a bonfire (see www.checkitsalright.nz) and let the kids collect and stack the soft, flat stones.

Hidden gem
The Ōkārito Trig Walk is a great walk for families — around 2 hours return with little feet, but older kids can do it faster, at 1.5 hours. The trig provides fabulous views of where the rugged coast meets the protected coastal lagoon and rainforest.

Experience
Go on a magical night-kayaking tour in the serene waters of Ōkārito to spot the elusive kiwi with Okarito Kiwi Tours.

Camp
Ōkārito Campground: One of my favourite places in this area. From the moment you arrive, it's a pleasant experience. The friendly volunteer hosts welcome families and take care of you throughout your stay. The camping spots are close to each other but not uncomfortably so. You can enjoy the lagoon and even drive your vehicle onto the beach for a campfire dinner.

Franz Josef and Fox Glacier

New Zealand's Glacier Country spans from the wildlife reserves of Ōkārito and Whataroa in the north down to the twin glaciers, Franz Josef and Fox, and the charming resort towns that share their names. It's a nature-lover's paradise, offering unparalleled access to some of the most impressive natural landscapes in the world, in one of only two places in the world where you can witness glaciers descending into temperate rainforest. Though snow is a rare occurrence in the small townships of Franz Josef/Waiau and Fox Glacier, the nearby mountains receive heavy snowfall, which is essential for producing ice.

Both glaciers are within the Westland Tai Poutini National Park, which runs inland to border the Aoraki Mt Cook National Park on the eastern side of the Southern Alps. The park is an incredible place that offers unforgettable experiences where the sea meets the mountains, and the landscape tightly follows the contours of both.

For hikers, the park is a true paradise, with numerous trails and walks that showcase the best of New Zealand's natural beauty. The park's temperate rainforests are largely untouched, and are home to many endangered species such as rowi (Ōkārito kiwi), kea, kōtuku (white heron) and tawaki (Fiordland crested penguin).

It is important to be well prepared before embarking on outdoor activities in Westland Tai Poutini National Park. To make sure your adventure is safe and enjoyable, keep the following in mind:

- Always check the current track conditions and weather forecasts at the Visitor Centre before setting out.
- The weather can change suddenly, so it is advisable to carry warm and waterproof clothing with you at all times.
- Don't forget to bring plenty of drinking water, insect repellent and sun protection.
- It is recommended to wear sturdy footwear, such as tramping boots, to avoid slips and injuries. Be extra cautious when walking on rocks, especially after or during frosts and rain, as they can be very slippery.

Explore

The Sentinel Rock Walk at Franz Josef Glacier is a short and relatively easy climb up a rock that was once under the glacier, being scraped by ice. From this viewpoint, you can see the glacier valley and the Waiho River, and information panels show dramatic photos of the glacier's retreat. This is one of the best places to appreciate the power of the glacier.

Nearby, the Peters Pool Walk is a short, easy walk through the breathtaking rainforest to a serene kettle lake, formed about 200 years ago by ice melting amongst glacial moraine. On calm days the lake provides reflective views of the glacier and mountain peaks.

Te Ara Kairaumati Walk at Lake Matheson, near Fox Glacier township, is a serene and picturesque trail that offers one of the best short walks in New Zealand. On fine days, you'll be rewarded with breathtaking views of the Southern Alps mirrored on the still and clear waters of the lake, including the world-famous Aoraki Mount Cook and Mount Tasman. Don't forget to bring your camera!

Experience
Get up close and personal with the beloved kiwi. Critically endangered populations of two kiwi subspecies — rowi and Haast tokoeka, which are the rarest of New Zealand's five kiwi species — are found only in the South Westland region. Head to the West Coast Wildlife Centre in Franz Josef/Waiau, the largest kiwi captive-rearing facility in the South Island, to learn more about these special birds.

Flying above a glacier in a helicopter, and even landing on the ice, is a bucket-list experience for many people. A scenic helicopter ride will take you up to witness breathtaking views of the glacier and the surrounding mountains before the icy fun begins. Choose from a variety of operators and tour experiences to suit.

Soak your adventurous bones in a private hot tub surrounded by forest at Waiho Hot Tubs. The specially lit fire that heats the cedar tub makes it smell really good. A fun and relaxing experience that you'll always remember.

Eat
The Landing Restaurant & Bar in Franz Josef/Waiau provides great home-cooked meals for families. It can get busy, so I recommend going early or reserving a table.

The last major supermarket for hundreds of kilometres is the Four Square in Franz Josef. It's advisable to pick up any groceries you need here before you head further south.

Cafe Neve in Fox Glacier has yummy, easy-to-grab cabinet food to fuel your road trip.

Bruce Bay Coffee Cart is a seasonal food truck located at a seaside lookout 50 km south of Fox Glacier. If you're lucky you'll see dolphins playing in the waves.

Camp
Orange Sheep Campervan Park: Convenient to the township and the Franz Josef Glacier Base. The grounds have basic facilities but are private and pleasant.

Franz Josef TOP 10 Holiday Park: Just outside of the township, offering quiet sites and excellent facilities.

Otto/MacDonalds DOC campsite: At the northern end of Lake Mapourika, north of Franz Josef/Waiau.

Fox Glacier TOP 10 Holiday Park: Good facilities including a kids' playground, games room and hot tub.

Hidden gem
On the coast west of Fox Glacier township, tucked away in a discreet

location, lies the charming Gillespies Beach DOC campsite. It is a true hidden gem. It is highly recommended to book in advance, as this place is in high demand. The campsite is situated directly at the beach, offering a tranquil atmosphere to unwind and relax. Fall asleep to the soothing sound of waves lapping against the shore, and wake up to the gentle breeze and calming scent of the ocean.

Haast

Haast is located on the western edge of Mount Aspiring National Park, and at the heart of the Te Wāhipounamu South West New Zealand World Heritage Area, which UNESCO has described as a significant natural treasure comparable to the Grand Canyon or Great Barrier Reef. Hunting and fishing are popular activities that attract many locals and travellers to the area.

Hidden gem
Jackson Bay is a small town located at the southern end of the West Coast road network, around 20 km south of Haast. Jackson Bay Wharf is a commercial crayfish and fishing hub, also popular with recreational fishermen who enjoy great sea fishing in the area. The bay also serves as a nursery for the rare Hector's dolphin.

Eat
You've got to try some whitebait. The Hard Antler or the Frontier Cafe & Bar offer a true local treat in an authentic environment.

The Craypot is a famous orange food cart located at Jackson Bay, literally at the end of the road. This small and quirky caravan-style cafe/restaurant serves fresh, locally sourced Kiwi dishes, including crayfish, fish and chips, whitebait, seafood chowder, burgers and more. Opening hours vary seasonally.

Camp
Haast River Motels & Holiday Park: The communal kitchen is spacious and well-equipped, providing a comfortable and cosy environment to prepare meals and socialise with other guests. The park offers easy access to the Haast River for fishing and other outdoor activities.

Freedom camp
Lake Paringa DOC campsite: 40 km north of Haast, this spot is perfect for boating, fishing and swimming in the lake. You can also overnight at the nearby South Westland Salmon Farm, and grab a coffee or snack from their cafe.

Haast Pass/Tioripatea Highway

The Haast Pass/Tioripatea Highway is a 140 km long scenic route that connects Haast and Wānaka in Central Otago (see page 281). This journey offers breathtaking views of high-country lakes, tussock-covered hills and steep mountains cloaked in rainforest. The highway passes through the third largest national park in New Zealand, Mount Aspiring National Park, where the forested section of the road provides an awe-inspiring backdrop to much of the drive.

Explore

Explore the beautiful natural wonders of Thunder Creek Falls, a 5-minute return walk that takes you through the stunning kāmahi and silver beech forest. An easy and enjoyable stroll along a well-maintained track leads you to the breathtaking 28-metre falls.

The Fantail Falls walk is also only 5 minutes return from the carpark, along a beautiful bush track leading to a stunning fan-shaped waterfall.

The 1 km return Cameron Lookout walk takes you through a stunning tawhai (silver beech) forest up to a viewing platform that overlooks the breathtaking Makarora Valley and the mountains around it.

The walk to the Blue Pools starts at the carpark located opposite Cameron Flat and takes around 1–1.5 hours to complete, meandering through tranquil beech forest, home to a variety of plant and bird species. The trail leads to a picturesque swing bridge that offers stunning views of the crystal-clear Blue Pools, at the mouth of the Blue River.

Camp

Pleasant Flat DOC campsite: A pleasant place indeed to spend the night, with well-maintained amenities. Enjoy the surroundings, including a short bushwalk and views of Mount Hooker.

Cameron Flat DOC campsite: Wake up to the morning sun in a peaceful setting to enjoy imposing views of the Makarora River and Mount Brewster.

Kidds Bush Reserve DOC campsite: With a day shelter, toilets and tap-water facilities, this is an ideal spot for picnics and camping. Spend the night under the stars after taking the short nature walk.

Canterbury/Waitaha

Nestled in a picturesque part of the South Island are snow-covered mountains, clear lakes and grassy plains. For those who have a deep love for adventure and exploration, the journey to Christchurch is a must. The city and its surrounds are known for their beautiful and blossoming gardens, fine wine and quaint towns offering relaxing hot soaks.

Explore the vastness of the region by visiting the stunning glacier lakes — the beauty of the surrounding mountains and the tranquil blue waters of the lakes will leave you spellbound. If you are a skiing enthusiast, the slopes offer an unforgettable skiing experience. For those who seek solitude amidst nature, there are hidden camping spots scattered across the region. These spots offer complete seclusion and an opportunity to connect with nature. You can spend your time connecting with the surroundings, enjoying a warm campfire under the starry skies, and feeling the peace and calm of nature.

Kaikōura

Following the main coast road (State Highway 1) south from Blenheim, you'll reach what could be New Zealand's most beautiful town, nestled where the mountains meet the sea. For us, Kaikōura was a true highlight, and if you're a fisher, you'll love it too. You can catch beautiful crayfish and blue cod, forage for kina on the rocks or head out for a dive. During our stay, we decided to drop some craypots while we explored the area for four days.

Kaikōura is also a popular eco-tourism destination, owing to the blend of marine wildlife that call it home. The giant sperm whale is the star attraction of the region, and also holds historical significance. The Māori ancestor Paikea was guided to New Zealand by a whale many centuries ago; today, Paikea's descendants live in Kaikōura and the whale still leads both the locals and tourists here.

Despite an increase in visitor numbers, and a major earthquake in 2016, the town has been able to preserve much of its historical charm and offers a variety of exciting experiences.

Explore

There are multiple locations in this area where you can observe the charming local seals. The seals are typically on the rocks and can be watched from afar, but in our experience they can be closer than expected, and suddenly emerge from nowhere. The best spots are the Point Kean Seal Colony/Kaikōura Peninsula Walkway and Ōhau Point, north of Kaikōura, where there are often baby seals.

Kaikōura is a great spot for your kids to learn how to surf or build confidence. Gooches Beach in Kaikōura township is the perfect place: located on the Esplanade, this beach is sheltered from the larger open-ocean swell, making it an ideal spot for beginner surfers. Another great place to surf is Ōkiwi Bay, just 10 minutes north of Mangamaunu. This small and quiet bay is known by locals as Sandy Bay, and is unusual because its waves break on a sandbar about 100 metres offshore. This makes it the only surf spot in the area where you can surf during onshore winds. For the best experience, surf at low tide.

Our family had a great time fishing together in Kaikōura. The kids enjoyed catching fish and discovering surprises while pulling up craypots with Dad in the beautiful water. The coastal area near the big drop-off is an excellent spot for fishing, and even smaller boats can venture into deep waters to catch fish. Try your luck and hopefully bring home some delicious butterfish or blue cod, known for their exquisite taste and beautiful white fillets.

Fyffe House, built in 1842, is the oldest surviving building in Kaikōura and is the sole remaining structure from the pioneer whaling station, in a breathtaking seaside location. It's right in the middle of the two-hour round-trip

walk along the shoreline that connects central Kaikōura to the Point Kean Seal Colony.

If you want to go for a dive, check out South Bay, on the sheltered side of the peninsula.

Experience the beauty of nature by taking the scenic and stunning Kaikōura Peninsula Walkway coastal track — perfect for families. Excite your kids by spotting a variety of wildlife such as whales, dolphins, seals and seabirds from the clifftops. You can complete the walkway in three hours, or choose from several shorter routes.

Experience

Whale Watch Kaikōura is one of the most popular tourist attractions in New Zealand. This coast is one of the few places in the world where sperm whales come this close to shore, due to an underwater trench running close by. As well as sperm whales, lucky visitors also often see humpback whales, orca, dolphins and seals, and the many seabirds that inhabit this coast.

Kaikōura is considered one of the best places in the world to have a magical encounter with dolphins. With Dolphin Encounter, you can witness the playful and athletic dusky dolphins in their natural habitat and even swim with them, an unforgettable experience.

Eat

For over four decades, the iconic retro caravan of Nin's Bin has been a landmark. The family-owned business, now in its third generation, serves up fresh crayfish caught using sustainable fishing methods. The recipe has remained unchanged over the years, with the crays caught early in the morning and cooked to perfection in a copper pot across the road. Served with a wedge of fresh lemon and garlic butter right by the ocean, the experience is nothing short of divine. Nin's Bin also serves up mouth-watering whitebait fritters, pāua and beer-battered fish and chips during the season. If you're in a rush, you can take a crayfish away with you, and they'll make sure to include a lemon with your order.

The Kaikōura Seafood BBQ is a shack by the beach serving mussel fritters and barbecued crayfish. Grab a glass of wine from the booze truck next door as you wait for your platter of locally caught seafood.

The Pier Hotel has a wonderful outdoor setting where you can enjoy the ocean breeze while indulging in delicious seafood chowder and sipping a cold beer.

Camp

The Store, Kekerengu: I highly recommend staying here. This campsite, on State Highway 1 north of Kaikōura, provides an experience that takes you back 20 years or more. Park right on the beach, enjoy the sound of waves crashing onto the shore — and maybe spot the local seals. Slowly wake up to the most stunning sunrise and take a morning walk to The Store for a good coffee and bagel.

The Point: This property, which has been passed down through five generations, is a special place to enjoy a camping experience that takes you back to basics. It offers a stunning natural campsite on the Kaikōura Peninsula. Listen to the waves hitting the rocks and enjoy the farm animals flocking about.

<u>Freedom camp</u>
Due to earthquake damage, there are only a few freedom camping spots available, at West End carpark, Jimmy Armers Beach, Scarborough Street Reserve (20 spaces), South End Railway Station Carpark and Pohowera (South Bay, closed over summer during the dotterel nesting season). Check specific times and details online.

Hanmer Springs

The drive to Hanmer Springs, from the south or west, is filled with mountainous ranges and vast landscapes. Due to its proximity to Christchurch, the town makes for an excellent day trip, but I strongly recommend staying in the peaceful village. This charming location is perfect for unwinding after long hours on the road. You can relax in the famous hot springs, or have a blast on the waterslides. For those with an adventurous spirit, the town has a wide range of nearby walking and cycling tracks that offer stunning alpine scenery, and there are some great places to camp.

<u>Explore</u>
If you are a walking enthusiast, Mount Isobel is a great destination for you. You'll need to set aside a full day for the trek. The Mount Isobel track is the most popular route to the summit, and it takes about 5.5–6.5 hours to complete the return journey.

The Forest Amble Sculpture Walk is a great walk for children, with many large wooden sculptures for them to discover.

<u>Experience</u>
Hanmer Springs Thermal Pools & Spa is definitely a great place for kids, but it's also a relaxing and soothing destination for adults. My family and I enjoyed lounging in the lagoons and even splurged on a private spa for some much-needed peace and quiet — it's the perfect place to spend the day. The kids didn't want to leave so we had lunch at the onsite cafe, which serves up delicious hot meals, ice creams and snacks, before jumping back in. The range of thermal pools available means there's something for everyone.

Take the plunge and feel alive with an adrenaline-inducing bungy jump off the historic Waiau Ferry Bridge.

<u>Camp</u>
Hanmer Springs TOP 10 Holiday Park: Adjacent to Dog Stream Reserve, just a short walk from the pools and the village, where you'll find restaurants, cafes, bars and shops.

Hanmer Springs Forest Camp: Great destination for those who love the great outdoors, surrounded by native bush and the comforts of a caravan park.

Freedom camp
Hanmer Spring River Reserve: Spot this riverside camp as you drive into town. Pretty views, grassy areas for picnics and restrooms. Arrive early, as parking is limited.

Amberley

Amberley is a cute country town that boasts a lively cafe scene, showcasing an array of delectable local treats. Its boutique stores offer locally crafted items, adding to the town's charm. Amberley takes pride in its agricultural heritage and supports local growers and producers.

As the gateway to the Waipara Valley wine region, the town is a hub for wine lovers. The Waipara Valley is home to a diverse range of wineries, each offering a distinctive wine-tasting experience.

Explore
Amberley Beach is a great place to take a leisurely stroll and soak in the views of the Pacific Ocean and the surrounding hills. The beach is a well-known destination among surfers, with its shingle beach and numerous peaks that offer both right- and left-handers. The waves are lively and fun, and surfers of all levels will appreciate them. At the north end of the beach, Fossils features a left-hand point break and beach break (though reaching it requires a four-wheel-drive vehicle or a long walk).

If you are here on a weekend, head to the Amberley Farmers' Market and experience the true essence of community as you interact with the local farmers and vendors and indulge in the range of fresh fruits, vegetables and other products. There are also some amazing food trucks serving delicious dishes and delightful crafts. It's a great opportunity to support local businesses and enjoy a day out with the family.

Eat
Brew Moon Brewing Company is a family-owned brewery and taproom which has been serving its patrons since 2002. Don't forget to try their delicious wood-fired pizzas, burgers and small plates that perfectly complement the beer.

Camp
Leithfield Beach Holiday Park: Great for families and right by the seaside.

Motunau Beach Camping Ground: A nice quiet place to spend the night, with unpowered sites and toilets.

Hidden gem
Napenape Beach is a serene and secluded destination which attracts the locals for surfcasting. To reach it, you'll need to take a 20 km gravel road leading off the northern part of Greta Valley. The beach is an ideal place to camp, on the cliffs with a breathtaking view to wake up to.

Crayfish pappardelle

With our freshly caught Kaikōura crayfish (see page 226), we made this simple yet elegant recipe that showcases the beauty of crayfish meat wrapped in fresh, velvety pappardelle. It's a great way to feed a crowd with just one crayfish. The pasta lets the crayfish flavour shine, complemented by sweet cherry tomatoes and chilli.

200 g (7 oz) unsalted butter
1 shallot, finely chopped
1 red chilli, finely chopped
2 garlic cloves, finely chopped
2 tablespoons lemon zest, plus extra to garnish
200 g (7 oz) cherry tomatoes
¼ cup dry white wine
meat of 1 crayfish tail, cooked and diced
300 g (10½ oz) fresh pappardelle pasta
2 tablespoons lemon juice
salt and pepper, to taste
bunch of flat-leaf parsley, chopped

Start boiling a pot of water with a generous pinch of salt.

Heat a large skillet over medium heat, then add butter and let it melt. Toss in the shallot, chilli and garlic with the lemon zest and give it a little stir. Add the cherry tomatoes and let them heat through for a minute before pouring in the wine. Allow the flavours to meld for another minute.

Scatter the crayfish meat into the skillet. If raw, cook it for 8–10 minutes until the flesh is white and firm. If cooked, heat it through for 5 minutes.

Meanwhile, cook the pasta in the boiling water until al dente. Drain, reserving a third of a cup of pasta water. Add this into the skillet with the pasta and crayfish, and stir to combine.

Serve the pasta in bowls and finish with a little more lemon zest, a squeeze of lemon, salt and pepper to taste and sprinkled with flat-leaf parsley. Enjoy!

Christchurch

Christchurch, also known as the Garden City, is a vibrant destination and a gateway to many South Island road trips. If you're planning to pick up your camper here, you might want to spend some time exploring the city before you hit the road. The inner city centre is easily walkable, and the rebuild following the earthquakes in 2011 has led to interesting innovations and fantastic community spaces.

Families with children will find plenty of fun things to do: take a tram ride down New Zealand's most beautiful street, go for a gondola ride to the top of the Port Hills, or enjoy a relaxing boat journey through the city and Botanic Gardens on the Avon River. Kids will also love newer, post-quake attractions such as the Margaret Mahy Playground, a huge fun-park for kids to explore, and the Transitional Cathedral, which is made of cardboard.

Explore
Enjoy the Christchurch Botanic Gardens on foot, or take a hop-on, hop-off tour in an electric shuttle. The gardens cover a vast 21-hectare area, with a diverse range of flora and fauna and different seasonal attractions.

Embark on a hiking adventure up Mount Pleasant, one of the most popular routes in the Port Hills, and enjoy a stunning view of the city lights at sunset. Although the hike is challenging, the reward at the summit is well worth it. Witness the magnificent display of pink and blue pastels, and orange and red hues that paint the sky, which is breathtaking every time.

New Regent Street is a must-visit location, offering a glimpse into the 1930s with its Spanish Mission architectural style. The street is home to a variety of restaurants, bars and shops.

Head inland and discover the fascinating geological history of the Kura Tāwhiti (Castle Hill) conservation area, on the way to Arthur's Pass. The limestone rock formations, shaped by centuries of water erosion, are a sight to behold.

Experience
Punting on the Avon River through Christchurch city is a beloved attraction that the whole family can experience. It's like a gondola ride in Venice, and offers a fantastic way to see the city from a different perspective. This eco-friendly activity is suitable for all ages.

Exploring the charming city of Christchurch is incomplete without taking a ride on the iconic heritage trams, which offer a fantastic way to experience the city's best sights. With an all-day hop-on-hop-off ticket, you can visit all the top attractions of the central city. The drivers are friendly and knowledgeable and provide informative live commentaries to keep you updated on the city's latest changes.

Kids

Orana Wildlife Park is just a 15-minute drive from Christchurch Airport and is home to New Zealand's only gorillas. Get up close and personal with the animals, feed a giraffe, witness lions roaming, and meet New Zealand's national icon, the kiwi. Orana Wildlife Park is an internationally recognised breeding centre for several endangered species.

Eat

If you're looking for a delicious food experience, I highly recommend visiting the Riverside Market. The market is located next to the Avon River in the heart of Christchurch, and has a vibrant atmosphere filled with exotic aromas and flavours. A variety of food stalls offer everything from aged cheeses and fresh vegetables to delicate pastries and handmade noodles. You can choose to eat right then and there or take something back to the van for later.

In New Regent Street, Casa Publica restaurant is a standout, offering an unforgettable dining experience. We loved their Peruvian fish. To end your stroll on a sweet note, head to Rollickin Gelato and enjoy a scoop of ice cream and a coffee.

Camp

Tasman Holiday Parks Christchurch: On the edge of the city, with a range of amenities including a spacious, fully equipped communal kitchen. There's also a spa and indoor swimming pool.

South Brighton Holiday Park: Peaceful location, surrounded by mature indigenous trees, and sheltered, private sites. It's on the edge of the Avon-Heathcote estuary, and close to South Brighton Beach, where you can relax or enjoy swimming and surfing.

Freedom camp

Marine Parade: A coastal carpark area available for four nights max.

Karaage chicken ciabatta burger

I love to make recipes that can be spread throughout a few meals. Making a large double batch of Japanese fried chicken is a great treat. I then use the leftover pieces to make karaage chicken ciabatta burgers, using the air fryer to reheat the chicken and crisp it up. The chicken gets double-fried — it's browned in oil, drained, then fried again to crunchy perfection. This recipe makes three burgers.

400 g (14 oz) skinless, boneless chicken thighs (about 6)
1 tablespoon finely grated fresh ginger
2 tablespoons soy sauce
2 tablespoons cooking sake
1 tablespoon mirin
1 litre (35 fl oz) vegetable or rice bran oil, for frying
2 cups katakuriko (Japanese potato starch), or use potato starch, corn starch or tapioca
sea salt, to taste
2 tablespoons Kewpie mayonnaise
Kaitaia Fire or other chilli sauce, to taste
mustard, to taste
3 ciabatta buns
3 slices cheddar cheese
lettuce, to serve
1 tomato
½ red onion, sliced into rings
burger pickles, to serve

Dice the chicken into 2–3 cm (¾ in–1¼ in) pieces.

In a large bowl, combine the ginger, soy sauce, sake and mirin, then add the chicken, ensuring the pieces are well coated. Leave in the fridge to marinate for a minimum of 1–2 hours.

Fill a wok or deep pot with oil about 4 cm (1½ in) deep and heat until it reaches a temperature of around 160°C (315°F).

Pat the chicken lightly with paper towels to remove excess moisture — this helps the starch to stick — then dunk it into the starch. Turn to coat well. Fry in batches for 2–3 minutes, draining each batch on scrunched-up paper towels.

Once the chicken is all cooked, skim any debris out of the oil and increase the heat to around 190°C (375°F). Refry the chicken for 2 minutes, or until it's crispy and golden. Once all the chicken is cooked, sprinkle with sea salt.

Prepare a sauce by combining Kewpie mayo, Kaitaia Fire and a little mustard.

Toast the ciabatta until golden before assembling the burger with chicken, cheese, lettuce, tomato, red onion, pickles and sauce. Serve with a good beer.

Tip
I check the temperature of the oil by dipping in the handle of a wooden spoon — you should see oil steadily bubbling around the wood. At the higher temperature for the second fry, the bubbles should be larger and rise more quickly.

Banks Peninsula

Banks Peninsula is a volcanic landform, carved into hills and bays with hidden bush areas. Even the journey towards the peninsula is picturesque. Akaroa (see below), Wainui, Okains Bay and Pigeon Bay are highly recommended if you're exploring the area. You can go for a hike or simply breathe in the fresh air while enjoying the beautiful scenery. It's only a short drive from Christchurch, but you'll feel like you're in another world.

Experience
Okains Bay Museum showcases treasures from the past, including taonga Māori and early Pākehā items.

The Fishermans Bay Garden is a popular spot for photographers, and a sensory feast that will leave you mesmerised by its vibrant colours and textures. Each garden area has a unique planting theme and offers stunning views of the Pacific Ocean. As you stroll through the garden, you'll be greeted by the sweet melodies of native birds. Take a slow morning to immerse yourself.

Hidden gems
Port Levy and Pigeon Bay are great spots for foraging for mussels on the rocks.

Camp
Okains Bay Campground: Classic Kiwi campground with well-equipped kitchens and two flying foxes, a climbing frame, swings and a slide for the kids.

Pigeon Bay Camping Ground: Back-to-basics-style camping with luxurious views and toilets, but no showers, kitchens or electricity.

Little River Campground: Bang for your buck! A great campsite which offers top-notch facilities like hot showers, an outdoor kitchen, barbecues, laundry facilities and even a seasonal herb garden. If you're travelling with kids, they'll love the Scary Slippery Slides, giant swing and playground with a trampoline, plus you can even feed the eels in the nearby river.

Freedom camp
Stoddart Point parking area, Diamond Harbour: A great place to spend the night and enjoy the turquoise waters. You can explore the area by taking the cliff walk to Church Bay to the east and Purau to the west.

Akaroa

An elegant town tucked in the heart of an ancient volcano that offers a one-of-a-kind blend of history, culture and natural beauty. The town's French heritage, combined with its rich Māori and Pākehā settler influences, is reflected in its architecture, cuisine and traditions. Akaroa is also an ideal destination for adventure enthusiasts and nature lovers, as it provides opportunities for activities like hiking, kayaking, swimming and wildlife

watching. Experience a range of excursions, from dolphin encounters to wine tasting, or simply unwind in an oasis of sparkling colours.

Explore

The Akaroa lighthouse offers stunning elevated views of the harbour. Head there for sunset and enjoy the sky's production of colour.

Visit the giant tōtara in the Montgomery Park Scenic Reserve, on the hilltop before descending to Akaroa Harbour. This magnificent tree is estimated to be around 2000 years old.

The Rhino Walk is a popular choice for families. Start at the Children's Bay carpark and hike through vibrant native bush, listening out for bellbirds and kererū as you make your way up. When you reach the top, you'll see a family of giraffes and the famous rhino sculpture, as well as views of the Akaroa Harbour. If you're looking for a longer walk, the Moa Point Walk continues on from the rhino.

Ōnawe Peninsula at the head of the harbour offers a breathtaking walking track that can be completed in under an hour.

Experience

Pōhatu Penguins is a local business run by a family that has been caring for korora (little blue penguins) for more than 30 years. They own a farm in Pōhatu/Flea Bay where the penguins live, and the guides are experienced and passionate about their work. They will show you the penguins in their natural habitat and teach you about their behaviour, habitat and the challenges they face. You can also take a sea-kayaking tour to see the beautiful coastline and other marine life.

Black Cat Cruises offer a wonderful dolphin-swimming encounter, with the world's smallest and rarest dolphin. The company is a strong supporter of and advocate for the conservation of Hector's dolphins through education and funding research.

Kids

Over 170 friendly and adorable alpacas live at Shamarra Alpacas near Akaroa. They love to make new friends and even enjoy being cuddled. Take your kids and say hello to these cute animals.

Eat

The Akaroa Farmers' Market, on every Saturday over summer, is the place to discover local producers in the area, with many growers plucking fresh produce direct from their backyards.

If you're a fan of fresh and locally sourced produce, Akaroa Butchery & Deli on the main street is a 'hybrid supermarket', as I like to call it. Whether you're looking to enjoy a seaside picnic or pick up dinner meats, they have an amazing selection of meats, local cheeses and Akaroa salmon. The shop also offers a wide range of European cheeses, pâtés, pickles, olives and award-winning olive oils that are perfect for a seaside picnic.

Akaroa is well-known for its king salmon production, and Akaroa Salmon is a top producer of high-quality salmon that is enjoyed worldwide. Their commitment to sustainable practices has earned them a global reputation and made them a role model for other salmon farms. Pick up some of their fresh fish from the Akaroa butchery.

Camp

Duvauchelle Holiday Park: We were greeted with warm smiles upon arrival and our campsite was a lovely spot located on the water's edge in Duvauchelle, at the head of the Akaroa Harbour. Two large, level terraces, with powered and non-powered sites.

Akaroa TOP 10 Holiday Park: A great base camp from which to explore Akaroa, with a heated swimming pool, TV and games room, toddler playroom and an outdoor gas barbecue plus a fully equipped camp kitchen, clean toilets and showers.

South Canterbury

Rakaia Gorge

Rakaia Gorge was a spur-of-the-moment choice for us, and we were delighted with what we discovered. After spending a few days in the city, we decided to take our Kombi and head towards the gorge. It took us around an hour to reach our destination, and we were immediately struck by the stunning views and vibrant colours of the Rakaia River.

This area is en route to Mt Hutt Ski Area, but it is also a beautiful place in its own right to explore and unwind. There is so much to see and do here, from hiking and fishing (mostly salmon!) to simply taking in the gorgeous scenery. Whether you are an outdoor enthusiast or simply looking for a peaceful getaway, Rakaia Gorge is definitely worth a visit.

Explore
Enjoy the river's edge for a picnic or a walk. Our kids loved rock-stacking and playing on the shore.

The Rakaia is a big, winding waterway fed by melting glaciers. From November to March, salmon swim up the river to lay their eggs, and trout also live in the river all year round. The best trout fishing is in the small, clear tributaries or in the lower parts of the river, where sea-run trout can be found. January to March is the best time to fish for salmon in the upper parts of the river.

Camp
Rakaia Gorge Campground: Overlooking the river, immediately south of the bridge. Well-manicured lawns and clean toilets, and a dump station. Open summer only, and cash only.

Methven

As we approached Methven, we were awestruck by the breathtaking scenery surrounding the town. Upon arrival, we were made to feel right at home.

Methven is a base-camp destination for skiers heading up Mount Hutt. The town itself is charming, with a bustling atmosphere that's hard not to love. In the winter, the place is buzzing with activity, thanks to the magnificent nearby ski area, but even at other times of the year, there's no shortage of adventure to be had, from jet boating and hot-air ballooning to scenic flights and mountain-biking.

Experience
As we drove into this quaint snowy village, we spotted a hot pools sign, and we jumped at the chance of soaking in the natural springs. Bookings were essential, so we made a reservation for the following day. Ōpuke Thermal Pools and Spa is a hot-pool paradise that made us feel like we had taken a trip to

the Swiss Alps. While we enjoyed the family area, we also noticed the adults-only section. Wouldn't that be nice? Apparently there is a swim-up bar . . .

Mount Hutt Ski Area is Canterbury's favourite snowy escape, boasting stunning views, excellent terrain and a family-friendly atmosphere. With a wide range of slopes suitable for skiers and snowboarders of all levels, from beginners to experts, the ski area features four chairlifts and one surface lift, and the longest run is 2.7 km. For the new kids, the ski area has an excellent ski school that offers lessons for all ages and abilities. The friendly and highly qualified instructors ensure that you get the most out of your experience.

Eat
During our stay, we discovered two great coffee shops. The first was Primo E Secundo, which had a captivating atmosphere. It was serving Allpress coffee, and while waiting we were kept entertained by the displays of second-hand goods scattered throughout the store. It felt like I was sitting in someone's cosy home, which I really enjoyed. The menu was filled with wholesome dishes and muffins, and my kids thoroughly enjoyed their fluffies.

The other was Topp Country Cafe, a corner store with friendly and cheerful staff. Our kids had a great time in the play area and we also tried their scrumptious scones with jam. The cafe is adorned with images of the Topp Twins . . . turns out, they own it!

Camp
Methven Camping Ground: Upon arrival, we were warmly greeted by the hosts and efficiently directed to our spacious grassy site. The communal area provided a great opportunity to meet fellow travellers. Additionally, it's conveniently close to the township.

Ashburton Lakes

Ashburton Lakes is one of my favourite locations in the south. As you approach the area, it's wise to take it slow, as you may come across herds of roaming sheep, which is quite a sight to see — it's like a scene right out of the *Country Calendar* TV show. This place is a step back in time, with limited phone and internet service, but that's what makes it so special. You get to enjoy dinner over the fire, breathe in the clear, clean air, and take in the beautiful surroundings undisturbed. We've been here several times, parking in different freedom campsites to fully explore the park.

Hidden gem
If you need a quick break, stop by the Mount Somers general store for a coffee and a hot pie. The pub around the corner is also a must-visit spot, with its friendly owner. Their bottles of wine are very reasonable, and they saved the day when I realised I forgot to bring wine to cook my ragù. Once you are out

camping in the Lake Clearwater area cafes there are no cafes or food stores.

Explore

Witness the awe-inspiring beauty of Mount Sunday, which provides magnificent views of the Rangitata River and the nearby mountains. It doubled for Edoras in the *The Lord of the Rings* movie series, and is frequently visited by dedicated fans.

Lake Emma is a picturesque location that offers a great opportunity to take a stroll and enjoy a picnic.

Camp

Lake Camp: A popular free campsite that offers incredible views of the lake and mountains. We visited in both summer and winter and enjoyed a winter campfire (always check if it's allowed — see www.checkitsalright.nz). Toilets have been recently installed near each entry, making it a comfortable and convenient camping spot.

Lake Clearwater: Located just a stone's throw from Lake Camp. A beloved recreational area for Cantabrians, with its village of holiday homes. The campground itself is beautifully grassy, with an honesty box for your fees.

Geraldine

The charming town of Geraldine boasts a warm welcome with plenty of character. Renowned for producing some of the country's best jam, Barker's is a beloved Kiwi brand based in the town. However, there's more to Geraldine than its delicious preserves. The town is a delightful place to explore, with an array of quaint boutiques, charming cafes and a pristine river that's perfect for picnics. Whether you're a foodie, a nature lover or simply passing through, it's a lovely place to stop.

Camp

Farmyard Holiday Park: A farm stay like no other, where you can enjoy a cosy campfire as well as the comforts offered by a caravan park. Children will love the variety of animals including wallabies, donkeys, alpacas, llamas, goats, kunekune pigs, Highland cattle, cows and sheep.

Orari Campsite: Explore the old bush tramway at this campsite surrounded by remnant forest.

Geraldine TOP 10 Holiday Park: Five-star amenities and vast open spaces.

Fairlie

Fairlie is a town that you should definitely not miss. Take a break and visit Fairlie Bakehouse to try their famous pies, or stay overnight and enjoy the beautiful sunsets.

Hidden gem
Burkes Pass (on State Highway 8) is a charming little settlement that is home to the Three Creeks arts and crafts store. As you stroll through the town, you will feel like you have stepped into a movie set. Take some fun snaps at the 1950s petrol station, admire the quaint blacksmith or browse through a collection of vintage memorabilia in the shop. Across the road is the first pioneer church that was built in the vast Mackenzie District, back in 1872. The church is beautifully preserved and is the perfect spot for a picnic.

Camp
Fairlie Holiday Park: A picturesque natural setting, surrounded by mature trees.

Lake Tekapo

From the moment I laid eyes on this breathtaking destination, I knew it would hold a place in my heart forever. Tekapo is a special place for any stargazing enthusiast, as it is part of the Aoraki Mackenzie International Dark Sky Reserve. This makes it the perfect spot to set up camp and spend a night under the stars.

Explore
I highly recommend grabbing a good book and heading to the Tekapo lakefront. It's a joyous place to visit whether you're there in the summer or winter. Kids can skip rocks on the glassy lake surface while the adults enjoy the scenery. This is also where the famous coloured lupins grow during the late summer months.

At the lakefront, you can't miss the charming Church of the Good Shepherd. The altar window provides a picturesque view of the lake and Southern Alps. The church was constructed in 1935 for the pioneer families of the Mackenzie district and is still used as a place of worship, but you can take a stroll around the church and admire its façade. At sunset, it is even more stunning — there are often photographers patiently waiting with tripods to capture the perfect image.

Experience
Whenever we hear that there are hot pools, we stop. Tekapo Springs is a family-run business with a rich history. Part of the farm overlooking the lake has been transformed into a series of terraced pools with varying temperatures, a kids/toddler area and, depending on the season, an ice skating rink, snow toboggan run and giant outdoor playground. You can also go at night and lay back in the pools, taking in the sky's magnificence. The cafe serves excellent coffee and good food, making it easy to spend an entire day here.

Our son is particularly passionate about astronomy, and the Mount John Observatory, located just 8 km from Lake Tekapo township, provides an

excellent opportunity to explore the past and present of the solar system. There is a cafe on site but you can only visit the observatory on an organised tour through Dark Sky Project.

Eat
The Better Batter food truck, located on Lakeside Drive, is quite the treat. This little vintage van sells sensationally crispy battered fish, popcorn chicken and squid to enjoy while you take in the pastel waters of the lake.

The Greedy Cow is a lovely cafe located on the main strip of Tekapo township. It can get busy at times, but I highly recommend being patient and waiting in line. The food is always fresh and delicious. If you're in a hurry, grab something from the cabinet along with your coffee and enjoy it by the lake.

Camp
Lakes Edge Holiday Park: Modern facilities and cool sites with lake views.

Aoraki Mount Cook

The stunning Lake Pukaki appears as if a bucket of pale blue paint was poured into the water, giving it a turquoise hue that almost seems unreal. This gorgeous colouring of the lake is due to the presence of glacial flour, composed of extremely fine rock particles that have been ground down by the surrounding glaciers. The lake is fed at its northern end by the braided Tasman River, which originates from the Hooker and Tasman glaciers.

As you journey along Lake Pukaki, you cannot miss the magnificent sight of Aoraki Mount Cook towering over its surroundings, the tallest mountain in New Zealand earning its moniker as the 'cloud piercer'. The breathtaking views from the various viewpoints along the way are nothing short of stunning.

For those who want to get even closer, hikes for varying levels of experience beckon. There are many other activities to enjoy here too, such as glacier excursions and alpine salmon fishing.

Explore
The view from Peter's Lookout is the most photographed road in the South Island, so come and take your own postcard. Views as far as the eye can see of Aoraki Mount Cook and the alps, as the road wraps and curves around the bluest lake.

When it comes to exploring, I always look for kid-friendly hikes that aren't too long. The Tasman Glacier area in Aoraki Mount Cook National Park offers a couple of great short walks, including the Tasman Glacier View Track and the Tasman Lake and River Track, both perfect for beginners and families. These hikes let you enjoy magnificent views of Mount Cook and the glacial landscape. Here's a fun tip: Send one parent ahead to hide some treats along the way. This lolly hunt will keep the kids motivated as they climb.

The Glencoe Walk is also a great hike for families, through tōtara forest with its ferny understory. You'll have to climb a little, but once you reach the top you'll be greeted with a breathtaking view of the Mount Cook Village, Hooker Glacier and Aoraki Mount Cook. Walk at sunrise or sunset to see the magic of the light falling on the mountains.

Experience

You can't miss the bright purple fields of New Zealand Alpine Lavender when it's in season. A great stop for a relaxing and fragrant experience.

Glentanner Park is a great starting point for those who want to fully experience the stunning beauty of these snow-capped mountains. You can take an exciting high-country helicopter hike and return to the cafe to enjoy delicious food, wine, beer and coffee.

If you are looking for an exhilarating and unforgettable experience in New Zealand, we highly recommend taking a ski-plane tour of Aoraki Mount Cook and the Tasman, Fox and Franz Josef glaciers — we went with Mount Cook Ski Planes and Helicopters. You will have the opportunity to land on a glacier and enjoy a picnic on the ice, as well as enjoying stunning aerial views of the glaciers and surrounding landscapes on the trip up and back. This incredible experience is truly a bucket-list-worthy adventure.

Eat

Find fresh and sustainable alpine salmon at the Mount Cook Alpine Salmon Shop, right by Lake Pukaki. We enjoyed the pōhutukawa hot-smoked salmon on rice thins with avocado as a snack, and it was also amazing in my breakfast frittata.

The Sir Edmund Hillary Cafe and Bar at the Hermitage Hotel is an excellent place to have lunch or a snack during your day of adventure. At the hotel, head to the Sir Edmund Hillary Alpine Centre, which is dedicated to New Zealand's premier pioneer, ambassador and humanitarian, one of the greatest explorers in the world. The museum displays the history of the Mount Cook region, including exhibits related to transport, climbing and Sir Ed himself.

Camp

Lake Alexandrina: A short and scenic drive to discover peaceful camping, picnic and fishing spots.

Glentanner Holiday Park: A special experience to camp in the bush near Aoraki Mount Cook. Hear the birds chirping and feel the fresh breeze while enjoying panoramic views of the mountains and landscape.

White Horse Hill DOC campsite: Camping under the mountains is pretty new to me — I am partial to a waterfront view from my kitchen window. However, this was an exciting twist to our adventures. White Horse Hill is at the start of several tracks; stay here for a night or two and wake up early to experience snow-capped mountains with your morning brew before going for a walk and returning to hot showers.

Freedom camp

Lake Pukaki is a freedom camping mecca. As you drive along the lake shore you will notice the many spots with parked vans enjoying the views. The Hayman Road site is situated near the power station, but don't let that discourage you. Drive in and explore the lower level near the lake edge. Check beforehand if it's safe to start a fire (www.checkitsalright.nz) and enjoy the breathtaking views of Aoraki Mount Cook.

Lake Pukaki: Beautiful straight-on view of the lake, with stunning sunsets. Near the river outlet off State Highway 8.

Baked BBQ Salmon

Lake Tekapo is famous for its fresh and tasty high-country salmon, which is raised in the pure, glacial waters of the Mackenzie Country hydro canals. My family adore this this barbecue recipe — it is one of our favourites.

1 side of sustainable fresh salmon, skin on
2 tablespoons dry white wine
3 tablespoons olive oil
2 lemons, sliced
4 tablespoons salted butter
bunch of dill
sea salt and freshly ground black pepper

Pre-heat the barbecue.

Place the side of salmon skin side down onto a double layer of foil and pour the wine at the base. Brush with the olive oil and place slices of lemon over the top of the flesh — this stops the foil from sticking to the fish. Cut the butter into knobs and place evenly along the fish, then place whole bunches of dill evenly over the salmon and season with salt and pepper. Bring the foil together lengthways over the top and seal the tails.

Place the fish on the barbecue grate and cook for 25–35 minutes.

Serve with salad or green veges, picking the salmon apart straight from the foil.

Tips
- I use salmon with the skin on, as the skin protects the base of the fish while it cooks.
- I like my salmon rare, so I remove it a little earlier than the recipe says and allow it to rest in the foil for 4–5 minutes. Salmon is so forgiving, it pairs with so many wonderful flavours and styles of cooking.

Twizel

I am a big fan of Twizel. The town hosts wonderful vibey markets and local farmers can be found enjoying their Sunday coffee in the park while the kids play on the playground. Visitors can stock up on groceries and enjoy a cool treat from Sweet Moos Ice Cream Parlour.

Near the town there are some absolute gem spots to enjoy for water sports, swimming, fishing and bike tracks.

Explore
Lake Ruataniwha is fun for families wanting a cool down, with great boating and fishing.

For all the passionate bikers out there, the Alps 2 Ocean Cycle Trail — New Zealand's longest Great Ride — starts near Mount Cook Village and runs all the way to Ōamaru (see page 290). The trail offers several levels and itineraries to suit different preferences, allowing you to take in the breathtaking views. Even if you choose to stay put and just admire the scenery along the route, you're bound to see many riders whizzing past with a smile on their face. The terrain is mostly easy to intermediate, making it ideal for day trips if you don't want to tackle the full journey.

Eat
The Musterers Hut: Tucked away just off the motorway lies a charming and whimsical cafe that is sure to delight anyone who stops by. The cafe boasts ample parking that can easily accommodate caravans, making it an ideal rest stop for travellers. The highlight of this hidden gem is the wonderful playground and mini-golf that offer a fun-filled experience for both kids and adults alike. As you step inside the cafe, the aroma of good coffee greets you, and you can indulge in a range of delicious beverages. The small gift store inside is perfect for picking up souvenirs or little gifts for loved ones.

Mint Folk & Co cafe in the township has great coffee and it's near the playground. Their breakfast burger is vibrant, just like the cafe.

Camp
Omarama TOP 10 Holiday Park: A great place to recharge and relax. I highly recommend checking out this lovely renovated campground: the hosts are super-friendly and welcoming, and there's a wonderful playground. If you're feeling like a soak, spend the evening next door at Hot Tubs Omarama in your very own private outdoor spa.

Lake Ruataniwha Holiday Park: Located south of Twizel township, on the southern shores of Lake Ruataniwha. Decent-sized campsites with good facilities.

Freedom camp
Lake Ruataniwha, West End: Free lakeside camping, with just the birds and bugs for company.

Lake Ohau Freedom Camping 1: The lake edge is all yours — enjoy the tranquillity.

Otago/Ōtākou

Otago offers activities and attractions that cater to all interests and ages. Breathtaking campsites nestled under mountains or beside crystal-clear lakes provide an unforgettable experience where you can connect with nature and enjoy the stunning surroundings.

Queenstown is home to a variety of ski fields that attract visitors from all around the world. The nearby towns of Arrowtown, Wānaka and Glenorchy boast panoramic scenery and renowned wineries offering wine-tasting tours and experiences.

Further south lies the vibrant city of Dunedin and the beautiful Otago Peninsula. The peninsula is home to amazing beaches that are perfect for swimming, surfing and relaxing. You can also explore the local wildlife, including penguins, seals and albatrosses.

Central Otago

I still remember the first time I drove through the Lindis Pass, which connects the Mackenzie Country with Central Otago. We were in an old station wagon and it was snowing heavily. We had to put chains on the wheels to make it through, so it was a beautiful yet scary experience. So as you can imagine I felt some nerves about coming back with a Kombi and caravan in tow.

Central Otago was the site of a major gold rush in the 1860s, and the Nine Mile Historic Reserve is a good place to explore as a reminder of the early days. It includes the ruins of the Lindis Pass Hotel and is a great place to picnic or camp.

As you continue through this historically rich landscape, you will also see the large merino sheep farms and fruit orchards for which the region is famous, and witness the dramatic contrast between the dry golden low country and the snow-covered mountains.

Queenstown

Queenstown is a charming and bustling town that offers a plethora of thrilling adventures, delicious food, exquisite wine and a vibrant social scene. This town has something for everyone, from adrenaline junkies seeking adventure to foodies in search of culinary delights. The picturesque views all around the town are simply breathtaking, especially during the stunning sunsets that are nothing short of a work of art.

Explore
The Seven Mile Point/Wilson Bay Track is a scenic hiking trail suitable for families, which starts from Seven Mile Creek and winds through a beautiful landscape of regenerating bush and pine forest to Wilson Bay, which is my favourite place for a picnic.

If you're a fan of *The Lord of the Rings*, you might be interested to know that the Ithilien Camp scene was filmed at Twelve Mile Delta, and also on Wilson Bay. Twelve Mile Delta is a popular camping spot, located at the outlet of Twelve Mile Creek.

Experience
RealNZ offers a chance to experience some of the most iconic attractions in Queenstown. One is the TSS *Earnslaw*, a coal-fired steamship that takes you on a lovely journey across Lake Wakatipu to Walter Peak Station. Once you arrive at Walter Peak, you can explore the farms and enjoy a beautiful lunch featuring the farm's own produce. The *Earnslaw* has been lovingly maintained since its construction in 1912, and is a symbol of Queenstown's rich history. During your journey, take time to explore the vessel, view the engine room and learn about the steamship's former life through the historic displays.

The Shotover Jet is one of the most popular activities in town, and it's easy to see why. These boats take you on an exhilarating journey up stunning wild rivers and through thrilling canyons. Brace yourself for an action-packed ride that combines beauty and power like nothing else. We sat on the lawn at Canyon Brewing and ordered pizzas and the yummiest beetroot karaage chicken. It's a great place to visit even if you don't feel like taking a boat ride through the canyon, especially on a lovely summer's day.

Kinloch Wilderness Retreat (Heritage Lodge), at the head of Lake Wakatipu, offers amazing guided kayak tours. If you're feeling adventurous, opt for a sunrise or sunset trip. You can also extend your stay and enjoy the lodge's restaurant and TV lounge, or explore the nearby walking trails.

Deer Park Heights is a beautiful and active farm that offers an enjoyable experience to visitors. As you drive through the farm, you will have the opportunity to spot goats freely trotting around, majestic Highland cows grazing in the fields, huge deer roaming around, and even adorable piggies. There is also a scenic lookout point which provides astonishing panoramic views of the surrounding landscape. There are several areas where you can sit down, relax and enjoy a picnic while taking in the stunning views.

Imagine yourself sitting in a cedar tub, in a room open to the sky, with a breathtaking view of the Shotover River. Every now and then, a jet buzzes past, adding to the excitement. This is the Onsen Hot Pools in Arthurs Point. The onsen hot-pool experience originated in Japan and is known for its numerous benefits. The warm and soothing water of the cedar tubs will rejuvenate your body and soul, leaving you feeling refreshed and energised.

Get ready for the ultimate thrill of a lifetime by jumping the Nevis with AJ Hackett, the pioneer of bungy jumping. My kids and I watched in suspense as my husband took the leap of faith from the highest bungy jump in New Zealand, at a staggering 134 metres. The jump lasts for 8.5 seconds, which may seem like a short time, but it's enough to give you a blitz of pure fear and excitement.

If you're a wine enthusiast, Queenstown is a great place for you. There is a wide range of exceptional wineries nearby, and I highly recommend embarking on a Queenstown Wine Trail tour to explore the local vineyards. These two regions are renowned for producing some of the finest wine in New Zealand, and a wine tour is the perfect way to experience it all.

During the summer months, head out on Lake Wakatipu for a paddleboard. With stunning views of the Remarkables and the other surrounding ranges, it's the perfect setting for your first stand-up paddleboarding experience, or for experienced paddlers. You can rent a board (or kayak) from Paddle Queenstown.

For an exciting winter experience, head for either Coronet Peak or the Remarkables. Both ski resorts offer a wide range of slopes and trails suitable for skiers and snowboarders of all levels. At Coronet Peak, you can enjoy stunning views of the surrounding mountains and valleys while skiing down the slopes, while The Remarkables has 385 hectares of skiable terrain. There are also terrain parks for snowboarders and freestyle skiers, as well as a tubing park for those who want to try something different.

Embark on a thrilling four-wheel-drive journey to witness the unique Central Otago landscape on the Skippers Canyon Scenic Tour, with Skippers Canyon Jet. A knowledgeable guide will accompany you on a trail that was hand-built by gold miners in the late 1800s, following the world-famous Shotover River. You will also get to visit the Skippers suspension bridge, the restored Skippers township, and a major *Lord of the Rings* filming location, The Ford of Bruinen.

Eat

There is an abundance of food options in Queenstown, ranging from New York-style pizzas, burgers and bakery delights to fine five-star sustainable meals. This place is heaven for food lovers! Burgers are a serious business here. You may have heard of Fergburger, but The World Bar also serves smash burgers that can certainly rival Ferg. World Bar has won the best burger in Queenstown award for a few years in a row and is still delivering. Their bacon cheeseburger and Korean fried chicken burger are not to be missed, and you really can't go wrong with them. The place also has great vibes.

Treat yourself to a night out at Sherwood. From the moment you step inside, you'll find the atmosphere is cosy and inviting, with dim lighting and comfortable seating. I highly recommend the mussels. And you can toast some marshmallows outside on the fire with the kids.

We found our coffee guy! Life's A Grind coffee caravans have become a beloved fixture in the area, and are the go-to spot for locals looking for a high-quality caffeine fix. They brew up the best possible Allpress espresso for devoted coffee lovers like us. Grab a caramel slice and a Pottery for the Planet keep cup while you're there.

The Altitude Brewing Tap Room has been making a name for itself with its flavorful selection of beers. Be sure to check out the food truck that's often parked outside. One of the most popular craft beers is the Foggy Goggles IPA, which is definitely worth a try.

Kids

Skyline Queenstown offers a fun experience high above the lake. You can choose from a variety of thrilling activities such as bunjy jumping, luging or taking on the challenging mountain bike tracks. If you prefer a more relaxing experience, simply order a glass of fine wine and enjoy the breathtaking view of the valley below.

The lakefront adventure playground is a delightful and engaging play area. With its winding slides, playful swings and a picturesque little river running through it, this playground is a perfect spot for the outdoorsy imagination to run wild. Parents can grab a coffee from the nearby Bathhouse cafe, which offers a stunning view of the lake.

Country Lane Retail Village is a delightful shopping destination just outside Queenstown that offers a children's play area, lush gardens and cute animals, as well as a range of locally owned and operated shops. The village also offers experiences such as beekeeping and honey spinning tours, beeswax wrap and candle-making, jewellery-making workshops, and guided e-bike tours. The village is committed to supporting the local community and is a treasure trove for those seeking one-off finds. Oh, and there's free parking!

We love taking our children to pools and aquatic centres as we travel, to develop their swimming skills and have fun in the water. Alpine Aqualand in Frankton is an excellent option for families, with two hydroslides, a fast one and a slow one. For toddlers, there is a safe and fun play area with exciting water features.

We almost lived at the very cool Hanley's Farm playground and pump track. The kids spent hours on their bikes and the flying fox, while we adults hit the outdoor free gym, which has a weight bar and boxing bag that is perfect for those living on the road. Bring your barbecue ingredients and spark up the park's covered community barbecue.

Camp

Driftaway Queenstown: A new campground on the edge of Lake Wakatipu in Frankton. The kids can have a great time in the indoor playroom or enjoy the outdoor bouncy pillow and playground, while the state-of-the-art kitchen is warm and cosy, perfect for those chilly winter nights. The barbecue balcony is a special feature, that feels like it is floating on the lake. The campground also has a baby bathroom and on-site hot pools that open up to the view. If you're looking for a place to eat, the Frankton Arm Tavern is just a stone's throw away.

Moke Lake DOC campsite: A tranquil campsite next to a small lake, tucked away up a valley. Boating, swimming, fishing and canoeing on the lake.

Twelve Mile Delta DOC campsite: Use it as a base for your outdoor activities, including boating, swimming and fishing, or exploring the walking and mountain-biking tracks that wind through the surrounding regenerating forest.

Glenorchy

I'd like to share with you one of my favourite spots in the area: Glenorchy. It's a hidden gem that's definitely worth exploring. It's just a short 45-minute drive from Queenstown, along what has been voted the most scenic drive in New Zealand, and is an amazing place to slow down and appreciate the breathtaking scenery that surrounds you.

The picnic spots in Glenorchy are some of the most beautiful I've ever seen, with stunning views of the mountains and crystal-clear waters — you might even mistake them for Austria! And of course, there is a *Lord of the Rings* location here too. But that's not all Glenorchy has to offer. This charming small town is home to a friendly local pub and if you're looking for adventure, there are plenty of options, from a farm experience to jet boating along the Dart River for an adrenaline rush. And if you're after a more relaxed experience, simply take a stroll through the town and soak up the peaceful atmosphere.

Explore
The drive to Glenorchy is always an adventure — our family discovers new hidden spots every time we go. It takes me back to those good old family road-trips when my grandma would pack a flask of tea and some baked treats for us to enjoy. One of my favourite stops along the way is Bob's Cove, near Twelve Mile Delta.

Lord of the Rings fans, if you're looking for a truly impressive location, you won't want to miss visiting the setting for the Isengard Lookout, situated in the majestic Dart Valley, just north of Glenorchy. The Dart Valley served as the backdrop for the dramatic Wizard's Vale, while Isengard itself was computer generated against the mountain ranges that create a mystical and imposing atmosphere.

Another nearby location is Lothlorien Forest. As you enter Mount Aspiring National Park beyond Glenorchy, you'll be struck by the incredible light and golden hues that highlight the various shades of green created by the ancient beech trees. In his novels, Tolkien describes Lothlorien as golden, ethereal and enchanted, which pretty much sums it up!

Experience
If you're looking for adventure, check out The Great Glenorchy Alpine Base Camp. They offer all sorts of exciting activities including snow camps. And for food enthusiasts, you must try the campfire meals — they're absolutely delicious!

The Routeburn is one of the iconic Great Walks, a highly sought-after hiking trail among both Kiwis and visitors. The eastern trailhead is beyond Glenorchy, and the hike itself is a multi-day walk that finishes at The Divide on the Te Anau–Milford Highway.

Eat

For a taste of local cuisine, head to Mrs Woolly's General Store, a cosy spot that serves up some seriously amazing kūmara and lamb pies. They also have a great selection of books and gifts.

Camp

Mrs Woolly's Campground: A charming and welcoming camping site that is part of The Headwaters, a not-for-profit community initiative. The campground is conveniently located in the heart of the Glenorchy township, just a short walk away from the picturesque lakefront and the lagoon boardwalk.

Kinloch DOC campsite: Across the Dart River dela from Glenorchy is a perfect destination for nature lovers and outdoor enthusiasts. It's right on the shores of the lake, and handy to the start of the Caples and Greenstone tracks.

Diamond Lake DOC campsite: A peaceful and secluded spot nestled on the edge of Mount Aspiring National Park. Take a dip in the lake and enjoy a refreshing swim, or try your hand at fishing for trout. For a more leisurely activity, rent a kayak and explore the tranquil waters at your own pace.

Arrowtown

Arrowtown is a charming, picturesque village located alongside the sparkling Arrow River and surrounded by majestic peaks. The village is a thriving community that offers great dining and shopping, and its heritage main street is a sight to behold, with well-preserved buildings and quaint shops. The area around Arrowtown also offers a variety of beautiful walking and biking trails suitable for all fitness levels. It's a New Zealand treasure that should not be missed.

The Arrow River originates high in the ranges and flows down to the Kawarau River in the Kawarau Gorge. After the discovery of gold in 1862, the river and its tributaries were extensively mined using alluvial mining techniques, which included hydraulic sluicing that left scars on the landscape, including tunnels dug into the hillsides to extract gold-bearing gravel. During all seasons, the river looks beautiful with its vibrant colours, and it's a fun activity for kids to forage for blackberries and walnuts along its banks.

Explore

The Queenstown Trail offers a multi-day bike adventure with overnight stays, or a range of half- and full-day rides that cater to different ages and abilities. It's an excellent way to enjoy the scenery with bike hire and shuttle transport available.

Discover the fascinating history of early settlers through their buildings, bridges and goldmining sites. Visit the Lakes District Museum, tour the Chinese settlement or take a short walk into the hills to see remnants of the goldmining days.

Lake Hayes Reserve is a peaceful spot where you can spend the day having

a picnic, watching ducks or fishing. Grab a wine and some cheeses from the Gibbston Valley Winery and enjoy.

Experience
The Royalburn Farm Shop offers a variety of farm-fresh goods, including sustainably grown fruits and vegetables, locally produced meats and cosy merino wool blankets.

Eat
If you're looking for a memorable wine-tasting experience, Amisfield is definitely worth a visit. Their cellar door offers a wide range of wines to tantalise your taste buds, which you can enjoy in their beautiful courtyard while taking in the stunning colours of Lake Hayes, or treat yourself to a meal in the award-winning restaurant.

Visit Mora Wines at Lake Hayes for a delightful guided wine-tasting experience. You can also relish a scrumptious lunch in the courtyard, which is beautifully festooned with flowers. Families with kids will love the winery's sandpit.

While strolling Arrowtown's beautiful streets, Wolf Coffee Roasters provides a great energy boost.

Ayrburn is the newest collaborative meeting place in Arrowtown, a one-stop eatery and wine cellar which is bustling with colour and vibrancy. This is the place to spend your Sunday completely unwinding, exploring local food, markets and enjoying lawn games.

Camp
Hampshire Holiday Parks Arrowtown: With its prime location, you'll have easy access to all the exciting activities and attractions Arrowtown has to offer. Top-notch yet affordable accommodation, and as a bonus, the camp amenities blocks are equipped with underfloor heating, ensuring a cosy and comfortable stay even during the chilly winter months.

Freedom camp
Kawarau Historic Bridge Car Park: Easy and quiet camp spot located outside of Arrowtown.

Cromwell

Cromwell is a tranquil town surrounded by mountains, on the edge of hydro Lake Dunstan. If you're a wine enthusiast, you'll love exploring the vineyard country and savouring some of the finest Central Otago pinot noir. For history buffs, the Cromwell Heritage Precinct is a must-visit, as it showcases the town's rich goldmining past. During the summer season, Cromwell is famous for its succulent stone fruits, which you can discover at the many fruit stalls along the highway. Plus there's plenty of room for watersports on Lake Dunstan.

Explore
Embark on your own journey around the wineries of the region. Mt Difficulty Wines is a must-visit — a beautiful place to enjoy hospitality while

taking in the breathtaking views of Bannockburn's dramatic rugged rock and thyme landscape. The cellar door offers an extensive range of wines, each with its own distinct flavour and character, with knowledgeable staff on hand to guide you through the tasting experience.

Kids

Kiwi Water Park is a popular summer destination located on Lake Dunstan. The largest water park in New Zealand, it offers a range of thrilling inflatable water obstacles.

My children had a blast cherry-picking at Cheeki Cherries during the short December season. We also plucked apricots and nectarines and enjoyed real fruit ice cream.

Eat

Tarras Country Cafe is a hidden gem on State Highway 8, between Omarama and Cromwell. This is a roadside stop worth pulling over for. Its warm and inviting ambience makes it the perfect spot to unwind and relish a delectable cheese scone, prepared with the freshest local ingredients. Additionally, next door you can find a real fruit ice cream parlour, a delightful sweet shop and a luxury gift store.

Camp

Cairnmuir Motor Camp: Located in a serene countryside setting, just 15 minutes from Cromwell, near Bannockburn.

Millers Flat Holiday Park: South of Cromwell on the Clutha River, offering a spot to recharge before continuing your journey by road or along the Clutha Gold cycle trail that passes the park.

Beaumont Hotel and Holiday Park: A classic country pub offering a small amount of camping sites. Beaumont is a small town on the banks of the Clutha River on State Highway 8, towards Dunedin.

Freedom camp

Lowburn Harbour: A large lakeside camp spot with lovely shady trees and plenty of other campers to enjoy a cuppa with.

Bendigo: Plenty of space, tucked alongside the highway with lovely lake views.

Jacksons Inlet: This is a lovely location in Cromwell Gorge.

Champagne Gully: Another handy place to stop and camp for the night above the Clutha River, between Cromwell and Clyde.

Wānaka

Wānaka is a lovely mountain town near Mount Aspiring National Park, offering easy access to the Southern Alps and a variety of exciting activities.

Adventure seekers will have plenty of choices, including canyoning, climbing, mountaineering and skydiving. The area also has many hiking and biking trails, and the crystal-clear waters of the surrounding lakes and rivers provide opportunities for kayaking, fishing and jet-boating. During winter, Wānaka is bustling with skiing and snowboarding activities, with four ski areas just a short drive from town.

Wānaka hosts a range of events throughout the year, including the Warbirds Over Wanaka air show, the Rhythm & Alps music festival, the Festival of Colour, and Challenge Wānaka, a scenic long-distance triathlon.

<u>Explore</u>
The Diamond Lake and Rocky Mountain Track is well suited to families with smaller children after something shorter and more relaxed. Overall it's a 7 km loop but a brief 10-minute walk will bring you to the serene Diamond Lake, then if you're looking for more of a challenge, head up to Rocky Mountain's summit. The trail can be steep and uneven in some places, so wear sturdy shoes.

Have you ever tried taking a plunge in glacial water? It's said to be great for your health! If you're keen for a refreshing dip, head to the Wānaka lakefront, where you can park your van for the day and enjoy the cool shade of big trees while your kids can have fun playing at the nearby playground. The main beach stretches over 1 km along Ardmore St, giving you a range of places to wade in. At the town centre, you can even jump off the wharf and swim out to the pontoon.

The charming village of Cardrona is located along the Crown Range road and has a rich history dating back to the late 1800s, when it was at the heart of the thriving goldmining industry in the region. Today, the historic Cardrona Hotel is a popular destination for campers and visitors, both in the winter as an après-ski spot and in the summer as a delightful dining venue with a large, sunny garden.

<u>Experience</u>
Experience the breathtaking views and tranquil environment of West Wānaka Station while horseback riding through the stunning backcountry with Wānaka Horse Trekking.

Wānaka Lavender Farm has 8 hectares of beautiful lavender fields, gardens and friendly farm animals. Take a walk through the flowers, play games in the garden and enjoy a cup of herbal tea or some delicious lavender ice cream. You can also try the farm's own Lakes Honey and other homemade goodies.

Winter sports enthusiasts must visit Cardrona Alpine Resort, which is great for beginners and intermediate skiers thanks to its wide-open trails. Experienced skiers will love the world-class terrain park. On the other side of the valley, Snow Farm offers over 55 km of trails for cross-country (Nordic) skiing and a fun zone where kids can enjoy snow tubing.

<u>Kids</u>
We have our kids' bikes and skateboards in our van for riding around town or

exploring parks. Our kids enjoy finding skate parks where they can spend hours practising their tricks. Wānaka Skate Park has recently undergone some upgrades, including a new pool-style bowl, a vert wall and a wave with a gap feature. It's a smooth and fun ride that kids of all ages will enjoy.

Eat
Wānaka's vibrant and diverse food-truck scene on Brownston St has such a cool vibe, where you can taste your way around the globe in one place.

Camp
Glendhu Bay Motorcamp: An authentic camping experience in a beautiful setting. Most of the sites are on the water's edge or have great views. The facilities are fantastic — one feature that I absolutely loved is the camp's eco-friendly approach towards waste management.

LandEscape Wānaka: Escape to a serene and picturesque destination. Their SpaGazer package sees you park your self-contained campervan right next to your own private, spring-fed, wood-fired hot-tub site.

Freedom camp
The Larches, Cardrona: A farm space to park and stargaze in.

Lake Hāwea

Hāwea is a truly beautiful lake just a 15-minute drive from Wānaka. Located on the road to Makarora and the West Coast, it's a quiet town surrounded by mountainous extremes, and home to some excellent fishing spots. This paradise offers a wide range of activities, including boating, swimming, kite-surfing, kayaking, horseback riding, walking and even just leisurely beach lounging.

Explore
The Isthmus Peak Track is a strenuous 16 km hike that takes you to the top of that mountain, which stands at 1385 metres. The trail provides breathtaking views of the Southern Alps, Lake Hāwea and Lake Wānaka.

There's an excellent walk from the Lake Hāwea township to Timaru Creek. This trail leads you through a beautiful valley of beech forest which eventually flattens onto a braided river bed. The magnificent views of the valley and the surrounding mountains make this walk truly breathtaking.

Camp
The Camp: An authentic South Island lake experience that has been attracting campers for decades. Beautiful simplicity and genuine charm.

Road-trip bounty balls

My easy coconut and chocolate balls are perfect with a cuppa.

1 cup desiccated coconut
1 teaspoon vanilla extract
1 tablespoon honey
1 tablespoon coconut oil
pinch of flaky salt
1½ cups dark chocolate drops
coconut flakes, to garnish

Mix the coconut, vanilla, honey, coconut oil and salt together in a bowl. Roll spoonfuls of the mixture into balls, place on a tray and pop in the fridge to firm slightly.

Melt the chocolate, in a microwave or in a double boiler. Using a fork, dip each ball into the melted chocolate and leave to harden on a baking rack or tray covered in baking paper.

Serve garnished with coconut flakes.

Otago Coast

Ōamaru

Ōamaru, located on the coast of North Otago, has charmed many visitors with its architecture and atmosphere. The town celebrates its Victorian heritage each year in November, and during this time you can see locals dress in Victorian style and enjoy some fun activities, including garden parties and penny-farthing races.

Apart from its architectural history, Ōamaru also has a number of natural attractions, including its little blue penguin colony and the limestone country inland.

Explore

It is always nice to enjoy community open space, so take a picnic or a coffee and stroll through Ōamaru's beautiful Public Gardens, one of the oldest in New Zealand, established in 1876. The lush gardens offer relaxation and a variety of attractions, such as the Craig Fountain, Wonderland Statue, Chinese Garden and the red Japanese bridge.

Discovering local artists is always a treat! Check out The Terraces Art Gallery on Wansbeck St for many amazing pieces. The gallery is housed in an old heritage building that's packed with local relics, so if you're into art or history it's worth a look.

Bushy Beach is a beautiful spot to observe the world's rarest penguin species, the yellow-eyed penguin or hoiho, at a safe distance, as they nest and play. Sometimes you can spot New Zealand fur seals on the beach here too.

Discover the wonder of Elephant Rocks, located about 40 minutes inland. These rocks are actually the remains of an ancient seabed that has been exposed due to tectonic processes, changes in sea level and erosion. Experience the beauty of these isolated 'elephants' that stand tall as a testament to the power of nature.

Experience

Ōamaru's Blue Penguin Colony is a great spot for families to observe these cute, waddling birds. You can visit during the day to learn about these tiny penguins, the smallest in the world, and see them up close during evening viewing times — check the schedule beforehand. These penguins have a lifespan of 8 to 10 years and breed on the coastal mainland and islands of New Zealand and southern Australia.

A great place to spend half a day is Steampunk HQ, an interactive museum in the Victorian Precinct, known for its unique sci-fi art, movies and sculptures. It opened in 2011 and has since become one of the most visited attractions in the town.

Kids

Ōamaru's 'steampunk' playground is located near the historic Victorian precinct and includes gymnastics equipment. A sealed walkway runs along the harbour frontage.

Oamaru Steam and Rail offers a nostalgic train ride every Sunday, weather permitting. The journey passes by historical landmarks and the clay cliffs near the harbour, before you disembark at the Red Sheds terminus. Explore the nearby restaurants and the blue penguin colony there; you can choose to return on the train or walk back to the town.

Eat

I absolutely love cheese! If my waistline permitted, I would happily indulge in a cheese platter daily. Luckily, New Zealand is blessed with an abundance of amazing cheeses. If you're anything like me and want to enjoy a charcuterie platter at sunset with a glass of rosé in hand, then you need to visit Ōamaru's very own Whitestone Cheese diner and deli. They also operate daily tours, where you can experience the making of — and taste — some of New Zealand's most delicious cheeses.

The Badger & Mackerel cafe is a warm and friendly place that offers a wide variety of delicious meals. They're famous for their iconic Kiwi mutton pies, and have a great range of cabinet food that can be taken away for picnics. I recommend trying the marshmolly cake, like a Kiwi lolly cake with sticky marshmallow on top! For breakfast, you can try their slow-roast pork belly Benedict, which goes well with great coffee.

For an unforgettable breakfast experience, Riverstone Kitchen, north of Ōamaru, is the place to go. This much-loved food destination presents a diverse selection of breakfast options that vary with the seasons, including breakfast bowls, smoked salmon and egg dishes. The food is genuinely delightful and well presented, but please keep in mind that the place is usually crowded as a result!

Camp

Ōamaru Harbour Tourist Park: A lovely, friendly caravan park with great facilities in a super convenient location, with all of Ōamaru township within walking distance. The area is quiet and peaceful, with friendly staff and good utilities. You may even spot blue penguins around the campsite.

Kakanui Camping Ground: Campsites on the edge of the Kakanui River, a 15-minute drive south of Ōamaru along the scenic coastal road. A great beachside location for families, where adults can surf and children can swim in the rock pools. You can also fish for whitebait in the Kakanui River.

Glencoe DOC campsite: Only a 20-minute drive from Ōamaru town centre, with plenty of space in a sheltered area surrounded by beech and podocarp forest, where you can enjoy walks and river swimming.

Freedom camp

Campbells Bay: A stunning location for outdoor activities like surfing and swimming. You can camp for up to three nights at All Day Bay, at the southern end. The beach has a surf break and safe swimming area. You might even see Hector's dolphins, but watch out for leopard seals.

Moeraki

Moeraki is a small village located on the coast between Ōamaru and Dunedin that is famous for the remarkable spherical boulders scattered around the shoreline. Sunset there is particularly beautiful. The town's name means 'a place to rest by day', and after just a few minutes here you'll understand why — this place is special and serene.

Explore

The star of the show, the Moeraki Boulders/Kaihinaki on Koekohe Beach are massive and nearly perfectly round rocks, which make for one of the most astonishing landscapes in New Zealand. Over 50 boulders are visible at this site. For the best photo opportunities, visit at sunrise or sunset.

You can find locals surfcasting from the rocks near the lighthouse, or follow their advice and head to Koekohe Beach.

Take a stroll to the 1878 Katiki Point Lighthouse, located on the southern tip of the Moeraki Peninsula. You might see yellow-eyed penguins and fur seals along the way.

Eat

Moeraki is a paradise for seafood lovers. The Fishwife, a well-known local restaurant, is famous for serving the most delicious battered blue cod in the region.

Camp

Moeraki Boulders Holiday Park at Hampden Beach: A charming Kiwi beachside camping ground with a mission to support their community. Lovely grassy and spacious sites make this a great place to settle in.

Moeraki Village Holiday Park: Close to the village, with a lovely vibe. Sea views and easy access to the water.

Trotters Gorge DOC campsite: A lovely and quiet bush setting that offers access to two riverside tracks, just south of Moeraki.

Dunedin/Ōtepoti

Dunedin is a city with a rich cultural history. It has a strong Scottish influence that can be seen in its architecture, music and traditions. The city is well preserved and has many historic buildings and landmarks that still stand today.

Dunedin is surrounded by hills and has a beautiful harbour. The Otago Peninsula, a short drive from the city centre, is a great place for nature lovers and is home to a variety of wildlife, including rare and endangered species such as the yellow-eyed penguin, New Zealand sea lion, little blue penguin and the royal albatross. The peninsula also offers stunning views of the coastline and the city. The landscapes are breathtaking, making it a great place to visit.

Explore

Allans Beach on the Otago Peninsula is a stunning ocean beach that provides a wonderful opportunity to observe marine life up close. If you're lucky, you can witness playful dolphins, adorable penguins and majestic seals in their natural habitat. The beach is just a five-minute walk from the carpark. Special wildlife such as sea lions often visit this beach, so take care around them.

Saint Clair Beach is a well-known spot for surfers, due to its consistent waves and breathtaking views of the Pacific Ocean. The Saint Clair Esplanade is a charming place for a leisurely stroll, with its lovely shops and cafes. At the western end of the beach, you'll find the Saint Clair Hot Salt Water Pool, which has been around since 1884 and is one of the few heated seawater pools in the country.

Hidden gem

Tunnel Beach, near Saint Clair, is a breathtaking natural wonder that has been shaped by the sea over thousands of years. The sandstone cliffs that surround the beach have been sculpted into a dramatic scene that is truly remarkable. While it may not be a hidden gem for those living in the deep south, it is still relatively unknown to many people!

Experience

There are not many chances in New Zealand to visit a castle — in fact, this is the only one! Larnach Castle on the Otago Peninsula is an important part of Dunedin's history. William Larnach, a merchant and politician of Scottish descent, built it in 1871 and today, the castle has been restored to its original Victorian grandeur. You can explore the castle's beautiful rooms and gardens, including a 300-square-metre ballroom that serves high tea daily. There are stunning views of the Otago Peninsula from the tower, too. Larnach Castle is located just a 20-minute drive from downtown Dunedin.

Eat

Good golly, Good Good is a fantastic restaurant that offers a vibrant and enjoyable atmosphere in which to relish a delicious burger and kūmara fries. It is a popular spot among locals and visitors alike, and the lunchtime rush is a testament to its popularity. The interior is a beautiful blend of vintage styles, burgers are cooked to perfection, and the kūmara fries and other deep-fried delights are crispy and flavourful, making for a delightful meal.

If you're looking for a delicious coffee experience in the heart of the city, OCHO (the Otago Chocolate Company) is a great option to consider. Not only do they offer delicious coffee (and hot chocolate, of course), but they also provide a fun chocolate experience with insightful information from the staff that is sure to delight both children and adults. Their dedication to high-quality chocolate is evident in every bite of their decadent chocolate slabs.

Camp

Dunedin Holiday Parks & Motels: A large and well-equipped park. The non-powered sites are on grass and feel like an oasis in the city.

Freedom camp

Warrington Domain: A highly recommended spot for freedom camping, right on the beach at Blueskin Bay, north of the city, offering stunning views of the ocean and surrounding landscape. Well maintained, with basic facilities such as toilets and rubbish bins. It's popular with both locals and tourists, so arrive early to secure a spot.

Taieri Mouth: Wonderful views and plenty of seaside air, south of the city. Enjoy throughout the warmer months.

The Catlins

Deep in the south, on the coast between Dunedin and Invercargill (stretching from Otago to Southland), discover a world away that is the Catlins. It's known as an explorer's paradise, with natural wonders that will leave you in awe. From the rugged terrain to the large tracts of native rainforest, the Catlins is a captivating destination that offers a glimpse into the unspoiled beauty of New Zealand.

Explore

Visitors from all over the world come to see the Cathedral Caves, in the cliffs at the northern end of Waipati Beach. The two sea-formed passages are about 200 metres long and can reach up to 30 metres in height.

The beautiful McLean Falls also draw visitors from far and wide. Located 15 km south of the charming Papatowai village and 2 km off the highway, the falls are a true natural wonder. A 1 km walking track winds its way through lush coastal forest, offering stunning views of the surrounding landscape before you are greeted by the sound of cascading water and the sight of the falls.

The hoiho or yellow-eyed penguins which inhabit the Curio Bay area of the Catlins are one of the rarest species in the world. Unfortunately, their population has declined due to the loss of coastal forest and the introduction of predators. However, much work has been done in Curio Bay to restore their natural habitat. Witness these penguins as they leave for the sea early in the morning and return early in the evening.

Jacks Bay, in the heart of the Catlins, offers stunning coastal views and some great walks. The bay has a beautiful beach that's perfect for family-friendly walks and spotting wildlife such as sea lions. It's also an excellent place to watch the sun rise. There's a cool blowhole 55 metres deep which gets going in a strong southerly swell.

The Pūrākaunui Falls are popular with photographers capturing the falling water. These falls are framed by native forest and cascade over three tiers — a height of 20 metres. The track is suitable for families, with pram access to the top viewing platform.

Head to Tautuku Beach, where you can take your coffee for a leisurely stroll down the estuary boardwalk.

Eat

The Catlins Inn in Owaka, the main town in the Catlins, had very cheerful staff to welcome us and the kids were delighted, playing in the toybox while we enjoyed the warmth of the fire. The special was a roast dinner, which was precisely what we needed after our travels.

Tumu Toka CurioScape: Enjoy a good coffee before exploring, and pick up some yummy treats to take with you.

Camp

Whistling Frog: The Catlins' best holiday park, located in a secluded area but with all the bells and whistles, and a lovely cafe.

CurioScape Campground: Camp in a picturesque site nestled alongside Porpoise Bay, with sites sheltered by alleys of flax. This bay is home to Hector's dolphins, which can sometimes be seen playing in the surf.

Newhaven Holiday Park: Easy access to Surat Bay, where you can enjoy a scenic beach walk to the nearby Cannibal Bay. The park's powered sites provide stunning views of the sea and are situated in a tranquil environment, perfect for a peaceful few nights.

DOC

Pūrākaunui Bay: Unlike anything I have experienced before. Be spellbound by this location. Wake up to breathtaking sunrises and enjoy watching a variety of animals in the morning while your campfire is blazing. From the edge of your campsite, you can witness giant sea lions playing along the beach, penguins waddling around, dolphins swimming and even whales jumping out of the water.

Papatowai Campsite Catlins Coast: Located in the bush and offers easy access to the stunning beach and estuary at Papatowai. There are also several short walks available nearby.

Southland/Murihiku

The southern region of New Zealand, known as the Deep South, is renowned for its jaw-dropping mountain ranges, national parks and coastal landscapes. The Fiordland National Park is a must-visit destination with its crystal-clear waterfalls, towering cliffs and majestic fiords. Southland is also home to Bluff, Invercargill, the Catlins and Stewart Island, where you can experience the warm hospitality of the locals. The bush and tranquil lakes provide an escape from the hustle and bustle of city life, and the many off-the-beaten-track walking trails offer the chance to explore the untouched wilderness. In winter, snow-covered mountains provide the perfect backdrop for skiing and snowboarding. The Deep South has something for everyone, whether you're an outdoor enthusiast, nature lover or simply looking for a relaxing getaway.

Fiordland National Park

Fiordland National Park, a UNESCO World Heritage Site, encompasses Milford, Dusky and Doubtful sounds. Milford Sound, hailed by British writer Rudyard Kipling as the eighth wonder of the world, can be optimally experienced through a scenic flight or a cruise. While some of the fiords can be explored by kayak, eco-tours can be arranged to venture to the less accessible ones.

The park is also renowned for its hiking trails. Fiordland National Park boasts three of New Zealand's Great Walks: the Milford, Kepler and Routeburn tracks. The Milford Track is arguably New Zealand's most celebrated walk. It spans over 53 km, offering incredible views of mountains, lakes and vast valleys, including spectacles such as the Sutherland Falls, the tallest waterfall in New Zealand.

Milford Sound is a breathtaking destination. It is a fiord that stretches for 15 km, surrounded by towering cliffs that rise up to 1200 metres above sea level. Milford Sound is a popular destination for outdoor and photography enthusiasts alike, adorned with breathtaking waterfalls, majestic summits and rugged terrain, making it a must-visit destination for anyone travelling to New Zealand.

Exploring Milford Sound is an experience in itself. You can take a scenic drive along the Milford Road, which is one of the most beautiful drives in the world, through the heart of the mountains and the Homer Tunnel to emerge at the edge of the fiord.

Doubtful Sound, also known as the Sound of Silence, is the second longest and deepest fiord in the area. More remote and peaceful than Milford Sound, it has several magnificent waterfalls, especially active during the wetter seasons. In the Hall Arm, visitors can witness the stunning sight of the Helena Falls cascading down the mountainside.

Camp

Cascade Creek DOC campsite: A picturesque camping spot that is nestled near the confluence of the Eglinton and Cascade rivers, just off the Milford Road. This location is a haven for fly-fishing enthusiasts, as both rivers offer excellent opportunities to catch trout. It's also the starting point for the Lake Gunn Nature Walk, a scenic trail that winds through lush forest and offers amazing views of the surrounding mountains.

Deer Flat DOC campsite: A standard camping ground on a grassy area beside the Eglinton River, surrounded by small pockets of beech forest.

Kiosk Creek Campsite: A hidden gem that offers stunning views of glacial moraine deposits and the surrounding mountains. The area is also home to a variety of bird species, including cheeky kea.

Milford Sound Lodge: Milford Sound's only campground, with limited spaces so you must pre-book. An exceptional camping experience where you can enjoy the tranquillity of the fiord, capture stunning shots of Mitre Peak or simply bask in the serenity under the mesmerising southern skies.

Te Anau

Te Anau is a charming town that serves as the gateway to Fiordland National Park and Milford Sound, but it also has attractions of its own.

Experience

Embark on an unforgettable adventure and discover the underground world of Te Anau with a guided glowworm cave tour with RealNZ. Your journey will take you across the lake then through a unique cave system that has been sculpted by water over thousands of years, creating a breathtaking natural wonder.

Experience the thrill of a seaplane ride and a scenic flight with Fiordland By Seaplane that offers breathtaking views of the world below, including some of the most remote areas of the national park. Take off from Lake Te Anau and fly over Milford Sound, Doubtful Sound or the Southern Alps.

Eat

You will quickly notice the craze for crayfish here, and if you have the means to drop some pots or go diving, then you might just come home with the goods. If you are looking to buy crayfish, the team over at Fiordland Lobster Company is dedicated to sustainable fishing and can hook you up with a tasty delight.

Cafe Ditto started out as a food truck and is now a busy establishment in the centre of Te Anau. We called in before our cruise in Doubtful Sound and loved it so much that we returned when we came back through. Try their tuna bowl: it is fresh and delicious.

Camp

Tasman Holiday Parks Te Anau: A comfortable place to camp located near the lake and town, with great communal facilities that are modern, recently renovated and, most importantly, clean and tidy. There's a kids' room and playground, too.

Te Anau Lakeview Holiday Park & Motels: Spacious grounds with plenty of camping options. Families will appreciate the full-sized bathrooms and helpful staff. Take a walk along the lake at sunset to see how pretty this area really is.

Kingston TOP 10 Holiday Park: On the road from Queenstown to Te Anau, this is a great holiday park near the bottom of the lake.

Freedom camp

If you're driving from Queenstown to Te Anau, make sure to stop and camp at some of the most beautiful lakeview locations along the way, including

Kingston Lake Camp, which offers stunning views and close proximity to the general store.

Lumsden freedom camp: A well-designed free camp with plenty of space, right in the middle of town near the info centre and playground.

Andy's Place, Te Anau: Outside of town, with grassy sites welcoming self-contained campers.

Manapōuri

Just a 20-minute drive south of Te Anau is the peaceful little township of Manapōuri, located on the shores of the lake of the same name. The lake has 33 small islands, countless bush-clad coves and numerous beaches framed by the majestic backdrop of Cathedral Peaks and the many layers of Fiordland ranges which span as far as the eye can see.

Experience
Visiting Doubtful Sound means embarking on the journey of a lifetime. It had been on our family's bucket list for many years, and we finally had the opportunity to experience it with RealNZ. The three-day adventure exceeded our expectations in every way possible. The sheer magnitude of the breathtaking scenes we encountered left us speechless. We slept in coves and woke up in awe of our surroundings, kayaked in waters that felt as if they could be home to dinosaurs, witnessed native flora in full bloom, and watched seals bask in the sea spray while perched on the rocks. Every moment of the journey was a feast for the senses, and we will cherish the memories forever.

Eat
Manapouri Cafe: While waiting for the boat transfer, enjoy the cute little cafe on the wharf serving baked goods and really good Allpress coffee.

Camp
We had an amazing stay at Possum Lodge before going on our cruise at Doubtful Sound. The location was like paradise, with stunning views and a peaceful atmosphere that made us feel like we were in a different world. Enjoy the lake and the lower Waiau River, surrounded by a beautiful beech forest. The property has a rich history, having been a campground for over a hundred years, and its humble and historical charm added to the overall experience.

Goodbye, New Zealand

The journey of returning to Aotearoa New Zealand has been very special and important to us. We wanted to show our children their home, reconnect them with their heritage, and teach them the importance of respecting the land they walk on. During our travels, we grew to appreciate the beautiful, untouched and ancient land of Aotearoa. We gained a deeper understanding of our Māori culture and developed a love for the native trees and wildlife. New Zealand has taught me to be a mindful person, inspiring me to make profound changes in how I eat, live and spend my days. Growing up I was taught by my grandfather that we are the kaitiaki — guardians or caretakers of the land, and that we must nurture and preserve it so future generations can enjoy it just as we have. It's been so important to share this with our children.

This book is filled with many of the beautiful places we found throughout New Zealand. Camping under the stars is an amazing experience that offers so many vibrant and thrilling opportunities. It provides the closest experience to freedom that we can get, so I encourage everyone to take a short or longer-term trip to discover the rare and stunning landscapes of this country. It's a chance to disconnect from the modern world and, in its simplest form, reconnect with one another. You can cook over an open fire, sip coffee on the beach and picnic in nature in so many amazing places. So, pack your bags and get ready for an adventure of a lifetime!

We are sad to say haere rā or goodbye to Aotearoa. We'll load the Kombi and caravan onto another ship and embark on our next journey, to explore the fascinating and culturally rich country of Japan. But we'll definitely leave a part of our hearts behind.

This is for you

To our children, Riley, Alba and Elsie, you inspire us every day to view the world with a fresh perspective. Your adventurous spirits have allowed us to cherish many sunny and snowy days together, and we are grateful for every moment. This book is dedicated to you as a reminder to fight for the adventures together and heartfelt moments that make life worth living. You have shown us that above all the possessions in the world the most valuable asset is time.

To Norm and Fay: although you are no longer with us, you inspired us to live life to the fullest and explore the world in a tiny van. There's not a day that goes by that we don't think of you.

To Nanny and Papa, I hope you read this and remember all the fun adventures we had throughout the years. I cherish all the memories and knowledge about my whakapapa (heritage) that you gave me.

Index

Abel Tasman National Park 199, 201, 202
Agrodome 130–33
Ahipara 73–74
Akaroa 244–47
Aldermen Islands 106
Alps 2 Ocean Cycle Trail 262 — see also bike trails
Amberley 231
Anaura Bay 147
Aoraki Mount Cook 257–59
apps 54–55
Arrowtown 277–80
Ashburton Lakes 251–53
Athenree 120
Auckland/Tāmaki Makaurau 78–91
    Auckland 80–84
    Matakana Coast 87–88
    Waiheke Island 89–91
    Waitākere Ranges 84–86

babies, travelling with 52–53
Banks Peninsula 244–47
Bay of Islands 61, 66–69
Bay of Plenty/Te Moana-a-Toi 118–41
    Katikati 120–21
    Lake Ōkāreka 135
    Lake Rotoiti 135
    Maketū 126
    Mount Maunganui 122–25
    Ōhope 139–40
    Papamoa 126
    Pukehina 126
    Rotorua 128–33
    Tauranga 122–25
    Te Kaha 141
    Te Puke 126
    Waihī 120–21
    Whakatāne 138–39
bike trails 99, 100, 108, 117, 128, 135, 138, 140, 167, 178, 186, 188, 212, 262, 270, 272, 277, 281 — see also mountain biking
biosecurity 23
Blenheim 188–89
Blue Springs 108
Bowentown 120, 121
breweries 62, 82, 87–88, 91, 126, 169, 176, 189, 211, 231, 270 — see also wineries
budgeting, for van trips 38–41
building a van 16
Burkes Pass 254

Cable Bay 73
Cambridge 111
camp life 44–47
campfires 47
Canterbury/Waitaha 224–63
    Akaroa 244–46
    Amberley 231
    Aoraki Mount Cook 257–59
    Ashburton Lakes 251–53
    Banks Peninsula 244
    Christchurch 238–41
    Fairlie 253–54
    Geraldine 253
    Hanmer Spring 230–31
    Kaikōura 226–30
    Lake Tekapō 254–57
    Methven 248–51
    Rakaia Gorge 248
    South Canterbury 248–63
    Twizel 262
Cape Reinga 74–77
Cape Runaway 146
Cardrona 282
Castlepoint 174
Cathedral Cove 100
Catlins 298–99
caves 62, 100, 108, 135, 201, 208, 298, 307
Christchurch 225, 238–41
clothing, for van trips 33
Clutha Gols cycle trail 281
Cook Strait 181
Coopers Beach 73
Coromandel Peninsula 96
Coromandel township 99, 100
CPD 'passport' 20
Cromwell 280–81

DOC campsites 46–47
dolphin watching 66, 148, 186, 211, 217, 220, 229, 246, 293, 295, 299
Doubtful Sound 302, 309
Doubtless Bay 70–73
Driving Creek Railway 99
Dunedin 295–96

East Cape 144

Fairlie 253
Far North 61, 73–77
farmers' markets 87, 96, 189, 194, 231, 246
Featherston 174
Fiordland National Park 302–7

fishing 62, 64, 70, 73, 77, 87, 89, 96, 99, 100, 114, 117, 120, 122, 126, 128, 133, 135, 140, 141, 144, 146, 148, 158, 170, 181, 185, 188, 220, 226, 231, 248, 257, 258, 262, 272, 277, 281, 287, 291, 293, 302 — see also trout fishing, whitebait
food, for van trips 28–30
Forgotten World Highway 158
Fox Glacier 206, 216–17
Franz Josef 206, 216–17
freedom camping 18–19
French Pass 188

games and toys 48
Geraldine 253
getting a van 16–19
Gisborne/Te Tairāwhiti 142–47
  East Cape 144
  Gisborne 147
  State Highway 35 144–46
Glacier Highway 206
Glenorchy 274–77
glowworms 62, 108, 111, 122, 135, 186, 208, 307
Goat Island Marine Reserve 87
gold mining 120, 207, 211, 266, 270, 277, 280, 281, 282
Golden Bay 201
Goldfields Vintage Railway 120
Great Coast Road 206
Greymouth 211–12

Haast 220
Haast Pass/Tioripatea Highway 222
Hahei 100–103
Hamilton 109
Hamilton Gardens 94
Hanmer Springs 230–31
Hastings 150–54
Hauraki Rail Trail 99, 120
Havelock 188
Havelock North 155
Hāwera 158
Hawke's Bay/Te Matau-a-Māui 148–55
  Havelock North 155
  Māhia 150
  Napier/Hastings 150–54
  Te Urewera 150
Hicks Bay 144, 146
Hihi 70, 73
hiring a van 16–18
Hobbiton 109 — see also Lord of the Rings locations

Hokianga 77
Hokitika 206, 212–15
homeschooling 51
hot springs 100, 103, 114, 117, 122, 125, 128, 130, 133, 135, 140, 203, 217, 230, 248–51, 254, 269
Hot Water Beach 100, 103
Huka Falls 114
Huntly 109

Interisland ferry crossing 181

Jackson Bay 220

Kahurangi National Park 208
Kaikōura 226–30
Kaitaia 73–74
Kaiteriteri 202
Kāpiti Coast 173, 178
Kāpiti Island 176
Katikati 120
Kauri Coast 61, 77
kauri forest 61, 77, 84, 106
kayaking 64, 73, 82, 96, 99, 100, 111, 112, 114, 122, 135, 144, 186, 188, 192, 202, 203, 215, 246, 269, 277, 281, 287, 302, 309
Kerikeri 66, 69
kids, travelling with 48–53
kiwi 64, 138, 164, 215, 216, 217, 241
Kūaotunu 99, 100

Lake Aniwhenua 140
Lake Hāwea 287
Lake Karapiro 108, 111
Lake Ōkāreka 135
Lake Pukaki 257
Lake Rotoiti (Bay of Plenty) 135
Lake Rotoiti (Nelson) 194
Lake Tarawera 135
Lake Tekapō 254–57
Lake Waikaremoana 149
Langs Beach 62
Larnach Castle 295
legal requirements for vans 18
Leigh 87
Lord of the Rings locations 109, 164, 181, 253, 266, 270
loyalty programmes 41
luge 133, 270

Māhia 150
Maketū 122, 126
Man O'War Bay 89

Manapōuri 309
Manawatū-Whanganui 162–71
   Ohakune 167
   Palmerston North 167–68
   Tongariro National Park 164
   Whanganui 168–70
Mangawhai 62
Mangōnui 70–73
Māori cultural experiences 66, 77, 128–30, 147
Marlborough/Te Tauihu-o-te-Waka 184–95
   Blenheim 188–89
   Havelock 188
   Marlborough Sounds 186–88
Marlborough Sounds 185, 186–88
Marsden Cove 62
Martinborough 174
Maruia Springs 203
Masterton 174
Matakana Coast 87–88
Matakana Island 122
Matamata 109
Matapouri 64
Matarangi 99
Matauri Bay 70
Maunga Hikurangi 147
meal planning, for van trips 32
Methven 248–51
Milford Sound 302–7
Milford Track 302
Moeraki 293
Mokoia Island 128, 133
Mōtū River 144, 146
Moturiki Island 122
Mount Aspiring National Park 277, 281
Mount Hutt 251
Mount Maunganui 119, 122, 125
Mount Ruapehu 164
Mount Somers 251
Mount Tarawera 122
mountain biking 100, 128, 130, 135, 166, 188, 212, 248, 270, 272 — *see also* bike trails
Murchison 203
Muriwai 86
museums 62, 64, 66, 73, 80, 120, 148, 149, 158, 168, 169, 176, 178, 186, 189, 211, 244, 258, 277, 290

Napier 150–54
National Park 164
national parks 44, 46, 114, 164, 166, 194, 199, 201, 202, 208, 216, 220, 222, 257, 274, 277, 301, 302 — *see also* individual national parks

Nelson Lakes National Park 194
Nelson Tasman/Whakatū 192–203
   Abel Tasman National Park 202
   Golden Bay 201
   Murchison 203
   Nelson 194–95
New Chums Beach 99
New Plymouth 158
New Zealand Motor Caravan Association 18, 19
Ngunguru 64
Northland/Te Tai Tokerau 60–77
   Ahipara 73–74
   Bay of Islands 66
   Cape Reinga 74–77
   Doubtless Bay 70–73
   Hokianga 77
   Kaitaia 73–74
   Kerikeri 69
   Mangawhai 62
   Mangōnui 70–73
   Matauri Bay 70
   Paihia 66–69
   Russell 66–69
   Taupō Bay 70
   Tauranga Bay 70
   Te Rerenga Wairua 74–77
   Tutukaka 64
   Waipu 62–64
   Whangārei 64

Ōakura 161
Ōamaru 290–93
Ohakune 167
Ōhope 139–40
Ōkārito 215
Okere Falls 135
Opononi 77
Ōpōtiki 144
Opoutere 106
Otago/Ōtākou 264–99
   Arrowtown 277–80
   Catlins 298–99
   Central Otago 266
   Cromwell 280–81
   Dunedin 295–97
   Glenorchy 274–77
   Lake Hāwea 287
   Moeraki 293
   Ōamaru 290–93
   Otago Coast 290–93
   Queenstown 266–72
   Wānaka 281–87
Otehei Bay 66

packing, for van trips 26–33
Paihia 66, 69
Pākiri 88
Palmerston North 163, 167–68
Papamoa 122, 126
Paparoa National Park 208
Paraparaumu 176
Pauanui 106
phones and wifi 54
Picton 186
Piha 84, 86
planning a van trip 24
playgrounds and parks 80, 89, 91, 112, 117, 120, 133, 135, 138, 140, 169–70, 174, 176, 181, 186, 203, 208, 215, 217, 238, 244, 254, 262, 272, 282–87, 290 91, 307, 309
preparation, for van trips 34–38
Pūhoi 87, 88
Pukehina 122, 126
Punakaiki 208
Pureora Forest Park 114

Queenstown 266–72
Queenstown Trail 277 — see also bike trails

rafting 114, 135, 138, 203, 208
Raglan 111–12
Rakaia Gorge 248
Rangitoto 82
Reefton 211–12
Rere Rockslide 148
Rotokākahi/Green Lake 135
Rotorua 119, 122, 128–33
Ruakākā 62, 64
Russell 66, 69

salmon fishing 248, 257 — see also fishing, trout fishing
sandboarding 74, 77
schooling 51
self-contained camping 18–19
Shantytown 211
shipping van to New Zealand 20–23
skiing 164, 166, 238, 248, 270, 281, 282
Sky Tower 80
Slipper Island 106
snorkelling 87, 99
Southland/Murihiku
    Fiordland National Park 302–7
    Manapōuri 309
    Te Anau 307–8
State Highway 35 144–46

stand-up paddleboarding 64, 73, 103, 106, 111, 112, 122, 126, 193, 269
Surf Highway 45 161
surfing 62, 70, 73, 84, 86, 87, 106, 111, 126, 140, 148, 161, 208, 226, 231, 241, 291, 293, 295

Tairua 106
Takapuna Beach 84
Taranaki 156–61
    Surf Highway 45 161
    Taranaki 158–61
Taranaki Maunga 111, 157, 158, 161
Tasman — see Nelson Tasman/Whakatū
Taupō 114–17
Taupō Bay 70
Tauranga 119, 122–25, 126
Tauranga Bay (Northland) 70
Tauranga Bay (Westland) 208
Te Anau 307–9
Te Āpiti-Manawatū Gorge 163, 167
Te Araroa 144, 146
Te Awa River Ride 108
Te Kaha 141
Te Mata Peak 155
Te Paki sand dune 74
Te Puia Springs 147
Te Puke 126
Te Puna 125
Te Rerenga Wairua 74–77
Te Urewera 150
Te Waikoropupū Springs 201
Thames 96–99
Tikitapu/Blue Lake 135
Tokaanu 117
Tokomaru Bay 146, 147
Tolaga Bay 147, 148
Tongariro Alpine Crossing 164
Tongariro National Park 114, 164
travelling with babies 52–53
travelling with kids 48–53
trout fishing 114, 121, 128, 135, 248, 277, 302 — see also fishing, salmon fishing
Tutukaka 64
Twin Coast Discovery Highway 61
Twizel 262

Uretiti 62, 64

van life
    budgeting, for van trips 38–41
    building a van 16
    camp life 44–46

clothing, for van trips 33
food, for van trips 28–30
freedom camping 18–19
getting a van 16–19
hiring a van 16–18
legal requirements for vans 18
meal planning, for van trips 32
packing, for van trips 26–33
planning a van trip 24
preparation, for van trips 34–38
self-contained camping 18–19
shipping van to New Zealand 20–23
travelling with babies 52–53
travelling with kids 48–53
working while travelling 42

Waihau Bay 146
Waiheke Island 89–91
Waihī 120, 121
Waikato 94–117
   Cambridge 111
   Coromandel Peninsula 96–107
   Coromandel township 99–100
   Hahei 100–103
   Matamata 109
   Raglan 111
   Tairua 106
   Taupō 114–17
   Thames 96–99
   Waikato 108–113
   Whangamatā 106
Waikato River 94, 108, 114
Waipara Valley 231
Waipoua Forest 77
Waipu 62–64
Wairarapa 173, 174, 178
Wairere Falls 109
Wairoa 149
Waitākere Ranges 84
Waitangi 66, 69
Waitematā Harbour 80
Waitomo Glowworm Caves 108
Wānaka 222, 281–87
warrant of fitness 18
weather and seasons 26
Wellington/Te Whanganui-a-Tara 173–73
   Kāpiti Coast/Paraparaumu 176
   Wairarapa 174
   Wellington city 178–81
West Coast/Te Tai Poutini 206–23
   Franz Josef and Fox Glacier 216–17
   Greymouth 211
   Haast 220

Haast Pass/Tioripatea Highway 222
Hokitika 212–15
Ōkārito 215
West Coast 208–11
West Coast Wilderness Trail 212 — see also bike trails
Westland Tai Poutini National Park 216
Westport 206, 208, 211
Whakarewarewa 128, 130, 135
Whakatāne 119, 122, 138–39
Whangamatā 106
Whanganui 163, 166, 168–70
Whanganui National Park 167
Whangapoua 99
Whangārei 64
Whangārei Heads 62, 64
Wharariki Beach 201
whitebait 158, 176, 201, 204, 220, 229, 291
white-water rafting — see rafting
wifi and phones 54
wineries 89, 148, 152, 174, 185, 188–89, 231, 265, 269, 277, 280 – see also breweries
working while travelling 42
'worldschooling' 51–52

zoos and wildlife parks 64, 80, 108, 176, 181, 241

Recipe index
Baked BBQ salmon 260
Camp lamb burger 136
Crayfish pappardelle 234
Fish tacos 104
Green-lipped mussels in red sauce 190
Healthy road-trip food ideas 30
Karaage chicken ciabatta burger 242
Peanut-butter brownie 196
Potato whitebait cakes 204
Raw fish 92
Road-trip bounty balls 288

Photography credits
Stefan Haworth, pages 142–43, 219, 223, 296 and 297 (top)
INTERFOTO/Alamy Stock Photo, page 175
Joshua Grimstock, page 292
All other photographs are by Lachlan Poole.

The information contained in this book is current as at the time of writing. Always consult the most up-to-date information online before visiting the locations mentioned.

First published in 2024

Text © Kirianna and Lachlan Poole, 2024
Images © Lachlan Poole, 2024

All rights reserved. No part of this book may be reproduced or transmitted in any form or by any means, electronic or mechanical, including photocopying, recording or by any information storage and retrieval system, without prior permission in writing from the publisher.

Allen & Unwin
Level 2, 10 College Hill, Freemans Bay
Auckland 1011, New Zealand
Phone: (64 9) 377 3800
Email: auckland@allenandunwin.com
Web: www.allenandunwin.co.nz

83 Alexander Street
Crows Nest NSW 2065, Australia
Phone: (61 2) 8425 0100
A catalogue record for this book is available from the National Library of New Zealand.

ISBN 978 1 99100 658 5

Text design by Megan van Staden
Set in Albra Book
Printed and bound in China by 1010 Printing Limited

10 9 8 7 6 5 4 3 2 1